I AM DIVINE. SO ARE YOU.

I AM DIVINE

DIVINE

SO ARE YOU

How Buddhism, Jainism, Sikhism and Hinduism
affirm the dignity of queer identities and sexualities

Introduced by

DEVDUTT PATTANAIK

Edited by

JERRY JOHNSON

Co-editors
Rev'd Loraine Tulleken & Rev'd J.P. Mokgethi-Heath

Contributors
Devdutt Pattanaik
Jerry Johnson
Sukhdeep Singh
Sachin Jain
Vivek Tejuja
Dr Meera Baindur

HarperCollins *Publishers* India

First published in hardback in India by
HarperCollins *Publishers* in 2017
A-75, Sector 57, Noida, Uttar Pradesh 201301, India
www.harpercollins.co.in

2 4 6 8 10 9 7 5 3

P-ISBN: 978-93-5277-485-2
E-ISBN: 978-93-5277-486-9

Typeset in Garamond by Special Effects, Mumbai

Printed and bound at
Thomson Press (India) Ltd

'Purush napunsaka nari va jiva charachara koi, sarva bhaav bhaja kapat taji mohi param priya soi.'

'Men, queers, women, animals or plants – any and all who approach me after abandoning malice are beloved to me.'

– Tulsi Ramcharitmanas (7.87ka)

Contents

The Intention of the Book

The intention of this book is to offer a personal perspective on how faiths based on the principle of karma – such as Hinduism, Buddhism, Jainism and Sikhism – can affirm the dignity of queer individuals. Karmic faiths reveal their theology not through authoritative books but through the individual cogitations of wise sages, rituals in important ceremonies, and through the practices of the laity. This book identifies a few of these practices, rituals and cogitations running across these faiths to articulate the manner in which they can be seen as lending comfort to the lives of queer people. This book does not intend to function as a philosophical treatise or a theological work of doctrine on these faiths. It does not intend to replace the voices of authority in the respective faiths or religions.

Disclaimer

This book does not claim to be academic, authoritative, comprehensive or definitive, but seeks to draw attention to the compassionate possibilities of Karmic faiths. The treatment of the topics herein is for a general reader interested in matters of faith, culture, diversity and queer issues, without requiring expertise or in-depth knowledge in any of these areas. The interpretations presented in this book are not intended to be prescriptive or critical. The authors of this book have more than a casual interest in matters related to faith, philosophy and theology as a guide to better living and have sought to share their personal opinions on the matter with the general public.

About the Title of the Book

'I am divine.'
'Aham Brahmasmi.'
Vedic Sanskrit. *Brihadaranyaka Upanishad*, 1.4.10. 800 BCE

'So are you.'
'Tat Tvam Asi,' which literally translates as, 'That's who you are.'
Vedic Sanskrit. *Chandogya Upanishad*, 6.8.7. 800 BCE

'Brahman' means the expanding human possibility, identified variously as mind, consciousness, imagination, intelligence, self or divinity in every living being. In later Hindu thought, 'brahman' is identified with *atma*, or individual soul, and visualised as God. Buddhists did not accept the idea of a permanent soul, or God. Jains accepted the idea of permanent soul, distinct for distinct beings, but not God. Sikhs speak of individual souls (*jiva-atma*) separated as drops of water from the ocean, which is divinity, the cosmic soul (*param-atma*).

Note: 'Brahman' is to be distinguished from 'brahmin', which is a Hindu caste; from 'Brahma', name of the creator god in Hindu mythology; and from 'brahmana', Vedic ritual manuals.

The cover image shows an 8th century carving of Ardhanareshvara, God as half-woman and half-man, at the Elephanta Caves, Gharapuri island, near Mumbai, India. This is a recurring motif in Hindu art. The male half embodies the mind. The female half embodies matter. This iconography also hints at the male and female principles of divinity present in all living organisms. It evokes equality of the gender binaries as well as a comfortable fluidity between the binaries, lending space to queer identities.

Definitions

Sexual orientation is an individual's enduring romantic, emotional or sexual attraction towards other persons. For example, heterosexual, bisexual and homosexual orientations range from exclusively heterosexual to exclusive homosexuality.

Gender identity is one's sense of self as a woman, man or transgender. This may or may not conform to the person's biological sex.

Gender expression is the outward expression of gender by, for example, behaviour, clothing, hairstyle, voice and body language.

In this book we predominantly speak of LGBT and LGBTI, but other related acronyms are LGBTIQ, SOGI or SSOGIE.

LGBT and LGBTI are people who define themselves as lesbian, gay, bisexual, transgender or intersex. It is a self-referential category.

Lesbian is a woman whose enduring physical, romantic, emotional and/or spiritual attraction is to other women. This does not imply any same-sex sexual expression or activity.

Gay describes people (e.g. gay man, gay people) whose enduring physical, romantic, emotional and/or spiritual attraction is to people of the same sex. In contemporary contexts, 'lesbian' is often a preferred term for women and 'gay' for men. Again, this does not imply any same-sex sexual expression or activity.

Bisexual is an individual who is physically, romantically, emotionally and/or spiritually attracted to both men and women. A bisexual person may be more attracted to one sex than another and this may vary over time. This does not imply physical or sexual expressions with people of both or either gender, neither does it imply multiple relationships.

Trans, transgender, transsexual and transvestite are umbrella terms for people whose gender identity or gender expression differ from those of the sex they were assigned at birth. They may include but are not limited to: transsexuals, cross-dressers and other gender-variant people. Transgender people may identify as female-to-male (FTM) or male-to-female (MTF) and may or may not decide to alter their bodies hormonally or surgically.

Intersex (previously known as hermaphrodites) is an individual who has an atypical development of physical sex attributes. These may include but are not limited to external genitals that are not easily classified as male or female. Or there may be incomplete development of internal reproductive organs. Some intersex characteristics are recognised at birth. Others are delayed until puberty. The term 'disorders of sexual development' (DSD) often refers to intersex conditions.

In the case of LGBTIQ, the 'Q' refers to 'Queer' or 'Questioning'.

Queer is a political term for all of sexuality outside of heterosexuality. It is often self-selected by those who either object to or prefer a non-gender-specific term such as 'gay' and 'lesbian'. The term has also been used to quantify those who go against normal convention, so it is not necessarily attached to sexual orientation and/or gender identity.

Words such as *'napunsaka'*, *'kliba'*, *'pandaka'*, *'pedi'*, *'kinnara'*, and *'kothi'* in Indian languages (Sanskrit, Prakrit, Pali, Tamil and Hindi) conservatively refer to the third gender (i.e., in terms of body or physical characteristics) but can also be liberally translated to include sexualities (i.e., feelings or psychosexual characteristics) across the queer spectrum.

Questioning refers to a state of being unsure of your true sexual identity but being willing to examine what it may be. This does not imply sexual expression or experimentation.

SOGI means sexual orientation and gender identity. For a deeper understanding of SOGI, please refer to the 'Genderbread person'. http://itspronouncedmetrosexual.com/2012/03/the-genderbread-person-v2-0/.

SSOGIE is a particular definition used by the Global Interfaith Network (GIN) for People of All Sexes, Sexual Orientation, Gender Identity and Expression.

Foreword

It may seem strange to many people that the Church of Sweden would be involved in the production of a book related to Karmic faiths. This is, however, not a book without a history. While many speak of an increasingly secular world, this stands in stark contrast to the living reality of the vast majority of people in the world where religion is part and parcel of every moment of every day; prayers are said at various times and moments of every day; meals are eaten after invoking the God who provides it. The vast majority of people in what some term the 'global north' are completely oblivious to the lives, faiths and realities of people in the rest of the world. And yet, as much as there is an assumption that the Abrahamic faiths reject homosexuality specifically and sexual diversity more generally, there is then equally the projection that this must be true of all faiths.

In February 2015 the Church of Sweden International Department supported the Human Dignity and Human Sexuality Stream of the Uppsala Festival of Theology. This Abrahamic interfaith dialogue resulted in the production and publication of the book *Behold, I Make All Things New*. It looked at the key issue of what the three Abrahamic faiths might say about sexual diversity. From the research done in this regard it was clear that the sacred texts of all three are not quite as clear on this issue as many would like. Historical context, linguistic interpretation as well as textual analysis provide a wide variety of views.

It was for this reason that it was felt that it would assist the discussion on human dignity and human sexuality to broaden the scope to include other world religions. Clearly, the Karmic faiths have a great deal in common. As you work through this book, you will find the many similarities but also the significant differences. Above all, you will see that the fundamental principle of equality is not a feature of Karmic faiths; rather, there is a celebration of diversity.

While it is very clear that through the processes of both colonisation and globalisation Karmic faiths have been influenced by the Abrahamic faiths, the differences can be clearly defined. Clearly, much of the homophobia experienced and practised in the Karmic contexts of India, Thailand, Cambodia, Myanmar, etc., is something which cannot be supported from a Karmic faith perspective. This in turn gives us new tools to look again at our own individual and faith community's reading of our sacred texts.

This book, written by scholars and practitioners of the Karmic faiths, seeks to guide you, the reader, into a historic and contemporary look at both sexuality and gender in the various Karmic faiths. As with *Behold, I Make All Things New*, the opinions expressed in this anthology are those of the authors and do not necessarily reflect the views of the Church of Sweden, the Church of Sweden International Department or of GIN-SSOGIE.

Our thanks go out to all who have participated in the research, writing and publication of this book. It is with great delight that we commend this book to you. We hope that just as this book has significantly broadened our own understanding of faith, it may both inspire and challenge you, the reader, as well. In our world we owe it to each other to understand more deeply the threads and streams of belief that both inspire and guide us.

Erik Lysén
Director for Church of Sweden International Affairs
September 2017

Note from a Hindu Leader

I am happy to hail this unique book. This is the first time, perhaps, that a book is born out of an inter-religious partnership in addressing the issues related to human sexuality. That, in itself, is a very significant thing and a sign of promise for the future.

The book espouses readers to look at the issues related to sex and sexuality spiritually. Indeed, it is a new way to facilitate readers to be faithful to their spirituality.

I congratulate the Church of Sweden and the National Council of Churches in India on the distinctive and substantial theological document that they have built up through their works. Today they are read and heard on significant issues across the country and the globe. The contents of this book will tell you why.

I appreciate the significance of the mission that has brought together these authors who are not only theologians or scholars but also simple faith practitioners from diverse religious traditions. They stand for the dynamism of true spirituality that affirms life, dignity and respect, and promotes a culture of inclusivity at a time when, in the wake of mounting discrimination and hate, the practice of religion is increasingly assuming an escapist orientation. The authors have spearheaded a proactive spiritual movement that refuses to be confined to religious ghettos and places of worship. The driving force of their spirituality is an unwavering commitment to social justice, to human dignity and the sanctity of life in its variegated forms.

The insights that the authors share with us through this volume are of enduring value, and the words can stand the test of repeated reading.

Religion teaches us to love. We need to learn the art of loving, lest we hate each other and call it religion. Spirituality, like life, is simple. We must be wiser in combating the campaigns of discrimination and hate. It is out of such spiritual keenness that this book is born. And I am happy to endorse it wholeheartedly.

May a culture of love and compassion spread all over the world and take hold of the hearts and minds of every person.

Swami Agnivesh
President
World Council of Arya Samaj
September 2017

Note from a Buddhist Leader

As humans, we have the unique ability to shape our own character with the choices we make. The responsibility of our karmic burdens lies squarely on our shoulders, and so does the possibility of our liberation from it. Being born gay or queer is only the beginning of a story that you have to write for yourself through your actions.

We have to train ourselves, therefore, to cultivate the four sublime states of mind (Brahma-viharas) and put them into action. And this is possible for all of us, regardless of caste, beliefs, gender, sexual identity or orientation. Liberation can be achieved by anybody. It is up to us to train ourselves to be ready for liberation.

Phra Maha Boonchuay
Chairperson, Asian Interfaith Network on AIDS (AINA)
Director, Chiang Mai Buddhist College
September 2017

Note from the Editor

At the outset, I must state that our collective debt to the ancient sages and thinkers of Indian philosophy is deep. Indeed, this book derives its core inspiration from their immense achievements in weaving colourful metaphors for complex philosophical ideas that now comprise the conscious and subconscious narratives of Indian culture.

This book is aimed at the lay reader and is our interpretative take on these narratives. After a brief introduction that outlines the broad themes of our topic, the main chapters of this book focus on the central animating principle of each of the major Karmic religions – Buddhism, Jainism, Sikhism, and Hinduism – namely, liberation, non-violence, equality and diversity, respectively. Together, these principles form the beginning of an affirming engagement with the lives of the religions' believers and practitioners, especially those who identify as queer or non-heteronormative.

There are too many people who contributed to make this book possible over the years.

I want to thank Roy Wadia, who first brought us to the attention of the Reverend J.P. Mokgethi-Heath and the Church of Sweden to take up this project. Their encouragement, generosity and support have brought this book to its completion successfully.

I want to thank Dr Asavari Herwadkar, who was instrumental in connecting us to key people to work on this book and for helping us get the endorsements of Swami Agnivesh and Phra Maha Boonchuay.

Indeed, meeting Phra Boonchuay was one of the many high points for me during the writing of this book. I would like to thank Phra for taking the time to review the chapter on Buddhism and for giving Asavari and me a guided tour of the major Buddhist temples and monastaries in Chiang Mai, Thailand.

Especially, I would like to thank Dr Devdutt Pattanaik, whose deep scholarship in mythology and Indian culture made him an invaluable consultant, contributor and mentor on this project.

My ability to edit and contribute to this book meaningfully is a direct consequence of the innumerable hours spent with Devdutt in conversation and exploration of the 'Big Ideas' from India.

Reverend Loraine Tulleken and Partho Sengupta were among the first persons to review the early drafts of this manuscript and help us sharpen our focus with their feedback. Siddhesh Inamdar from HarperCollins has helped take this book to its final, refined form.

As someone raised in a Catholic household, I was woefully ill-equipped to write a book about Karmic faiths and their interpretations of human sexuality. While my exposure to these faiths was substantive, it remained largely non-critical. Hence, the contributions of my co-authors Vivek Tejuja, Sachin Jain,

Sukhdeep Singh and Dr Meera Baindur are invaluable to the central themes of this book. The subjective perspectives about their own faiths and their lived experiences greatly inform the essays in this book and expand their interpretive scope.

Finally, this book is dedicated to all persons around the world, and especially in India, who find themselves feeling odd, queer or not quite fitting into the mainstream. I hope that through this book they find an affirmation of their uniqueness and the realisation that in them – as in all things – resides the divine.

Jerry Johnson
Editor
October 2017

The Key Players

GIN

The Global Interfaith Network for People of All Sexes, Sexual Orientation, Gender Identity and Expression (GIN-SSOGIE) was initiated by sixty-eight people from thirty-five countries at the 2012 International Lesbian, Gay, Bisexual, Trans and Intersex Association (ILGA) Conference. It was further consolidated at a spiritual retreat in January 2014 and a subsequent ILGA conference in Mexico City the same year.

The non-profit network was registered in South Africa in 2015. The secretariat is based in Johannesburg, which offers easy access to the rest of Africa and the other continents. In its first year, GIN attracted more than 300 members, representing six continents and eight faith groups, the vast majority being from the global south.

For more information, please visit www.gin-ssogie.org or email info@gin-ssogie.org.

The Church Of Sweden

On 22 October 2009, the General Synod of the Church of Sweden voted 176 to 62 in favour of allowing its priests to wed same-sex couples in new gender-neutral church ceremonies, including the use of the term 'marriage'. That same year Eva Brunne was elected and consecrated as the Church of Sweden

Bishop of Stockholm. She was the first openly lesbian bishop in the world and the first bishop of the Lutheran denomination in Sweden to be in a registered same-sex partnership.

The Church does, however, permit priests to decline to marry couples of the same gender, as is the case for heterosexual couples. The only special proviso made for same-sex couples is that every parish has a responsibility to make it possible for them to marry in it, regardless of the opinion of the clergy concerned. It was the first major denomination and religion in Sweden to approve same-sex marriage.

The vote for same-sex marriages also set the Church of Sweden apart from others within the Lutheran World Federation. The issues of same-sex cohabitation and the place of LGBTI people in the Church have been discussed and investigated since 1972. Notably, the Church of Sweden had permitted the blessing of same-sex unions and the ordination of partnered gays and lesbians since 2006. Describing itself as a folk or people's church, as opposed to a state church regulated by parliament, it embraces the whole country.

Thus, the focus is on ministering well beyond active church members and Sweden's geographic boundaries.

The Reverend J.P. Mokgethi-Heath

An Anglican priest, he is Policy Advisor on HIV and Theology for the International Department of the Church of Sweden. Having served as a parish priest in the Diocese of Johannesburg from 1995, he co-founded the International Network of Religious Leaders Living with or Personally

Affected by HIV and AIDS (INERELA+) in 2002 and served as Executive Director. By January 2013, when he took up his post in Sweden, the network had grown from an initial membership of eight to a global network with more than 10,000 members from all faiths.

Having tested HIV positive in 2000, when his immune system was already seriously compromised, he was blessed to be accepted for a medical trial that saved his life. In the following years he was burying people who had no access to treatment. Out of this emerged the internationally respected activist.

'It is universally recognised that religious leaders have a unique authority that plays a central role in providing moral and ethical guidance within their communities,' he says. 'Indeed, their public opinions can influence entire nations.'

Devdutt Pattanaik

Devdutt, a practising Hindu, has authored the introductory essay in this book on faiths based on karma. A consultant to the entire project, he writes, illustrates and lectures on the relevance of mythology in modern times. He defines mythology as 'subjective truth of a people expressed through stories, symbols and rituals'. He has written more than thirty books and 700 articles, including two based on queer themes: *Shikhandi and Other Tales They Don't Tell You* (Zubaan) and *The Pregnant King: A Novel* (Penguin).

A public speaker, leadership coach and management theorist, he is also a culture consultant with TV shows on CNBC-TV18 and Epic Channel.

Jerry Johnson

Jerry Johnson earned a Bachelor's degree in Communication from Roosevelt University in Chicago, with extensive academic work in Psychology and Philosophy. He also studied Political Economy in Latin America at the Universidad de Los Andes in Santiago, Chile, and completed the Philosophy of Political Economy (PPE) programme through George Mason University and the University of Hong Kong.

Raised in a south Indian Catholic family, Jerry lives as an openly gay man in India, championing human rights within a liberal framework, appearing on television news and various forums both in India and abroad. He is a TEDx speaker and curator and has published several opinion pieces in national weeklies and daily newspapers.

Jerry is the editor of this book and has written the chapters on Hinduism and Buddhism and edited the chapters on Jainism and Sikhism.

Sukhdeep Singh

He is the founding editor of *Gaylaxy* magazine, India's leading English language LGBTIQ magazine. His writings have appeared on other online portals like Huffington Post India, Varta, Ebab.com, Trikone Magazine. Sukhdeep was born and raised in a Sikh family.

He has written the chapter on Sikhism in this book.

Sachin Jain

Sachin is the Hindi editor of *Gaylaxy*, founder of Gay

Housing Assistance Resource (GHAR), a pan-Indian queer accommodation bulletin board, and core member of GayBombay, a gay support organisation. After working as a software engineer, he joined his family firm and obtained an MBA in international business. A Teach For India Fellow, Sachin has an MA in Philosophy, specialising in Jain Studies. He presently works as a Spanish teacher at an international school in Mumbai and is a practising Jain.

He contributed to the chapter on Jainism.

Vivek Tejuja

A literature graduate and a practising Buddhist, Vivek has worked with the content and merchandising of books as well as publishing for about four years. His own first book, *So Now You Know*, a sixteen-year-old's coming-out story in contemporary Mumbai, was published in December 2016.

He contributed to the chapter on Buddhism in this book.

Dr Meera Baindur

A faculty member at the Manipal Centre for Philosophy and Humanities, Manipal University, Dr Meera currently is the coordinator of the Centre for Women's Studies. She has a doctoral degree from the university in the interdisciplinary area of environmental philosophy which she completed through the National Institute of Advanced Studies, Bangalore. Earlier, she stayed with village communities in the Himalayas for a few years, working directly on environment and sustainability issues. During this time she also pursued traditional studies in Indian philosophy and yoga.

Her research interests include environmental philosophy and environmental humanities, gender and women's studies, and body studies. She has taught and lectured on traditional Indian philosophy, philosophy of religion, Hinduism, mythology and narratives, and her recent work centres on religions and ecological practice, women and sexuality in religious literature.

A practising Hindu, she contributed to the chapters on Hinduism and Buddhism in this book.

Introduction to the Karmic Faiths

By Devdutt Pattanaik

- What Are Karmic Faiths?

- What Are the Key Features of Karmic Faiths?

- How Do We Distinguish between
  Individual Karmic Faiths?

- What Is the History of Karmic Faiths?

- How Do Karmic Faiths Look at Nature?

- How Do Karmic Faiths Look at Culture?

- A Note on the Castes of India

- A Note on the Tribes of India

- How Do Karmic Faiths Look at Scriptures?

- How Do Karmic Faiths Look at the Queer?

- How Have Karmic Faiths Been Used to
  Be Hostile to the Queer?

- How Can Karmic Faiths Be Used to
  Affirm the Dignity of the Queer?

Kalachakra: The cycle of rebirths that is the fundamental metaphysical assumption of Buddhism, Jainism, Hinduism and Sikhism. *(Source: Wikimedia Commons)*

In the 20th century the doctrine of secularism has demanded that faith (or organised faith, i.e., religion) be kept away from politics, economics and identity. This has resulted in a fracture that has contributed to many social problems, including queer-phobia: the explicit and implicit hostility towards LGBTIQ people.

More and more people around the world are realising that the secular cannot afford to deny the value of faith in the lives of people. Faith helps people cope with fear. Faith gives meaning to people's lives. When faiths affirm the dignity of queer people, they empower them psychologically, which enables them to thrive politically and economically. By promoting inclusiveness and harmony, they also reduce queer-phobic tendencies in neighbourhoods where they live.

In this essay I will try to arrive at an appreciation of faiths that are based on karma. These are the Karmic faiths. These have long been misunderstood as they have been seen through the lens of Abrahamic faiths (Judaism, Christianity, Islam) that dominate global discourse on faiths. Karmic faiths approach the idea of queer very differently as it is not based on God's commandments.

Karmic faiths include Buddhism, Jainism, Sikhism and Hinduism. They are based on the idea of rebirth, hence karma. They do not subscribe to the belief that there is only one life followed by an eternal afterlife, or to Abrahamic notions of divine commandments, damnation and salvation.

Having originated in the Indian subcontinent (now increasingly referred to as South Asia), Karmic faiths have spread, mainly via Buddhism, to South East, Central and East Asia. Today, Karmic faiths thrive amongst 20 per cent of the world's population – mostly communities who live in India, Nepal, Bhutan, Sri Lanka, Pakistan, Myanmar, Thailand, Cambodia, Laos, Japan, Singapore, Taiwan and Hong Kong. Many people from these communities have migrated for economic and political reasons to the developed economies of Europe and America. And so we can say Karmic faiths are very much global faiths.

Increasingly, Karmic faiths are being known as Dharmic faiths, though the meaning of the word '*dharma*' in each of these faiths is very different.[1]

What Are Karmic Faiths?

Karmic faiths are based on the belief of rebirth: deeds of past life impact the current life and deeds of the current life impact future lives. Every entity is therefore unique, bound by its karmic burden, which accounts for the circumstances that make up its own life. This accounts for the diversity of the world. In this paradigm, there is no one to blame for one's situation in life. We are our own creations. And the choices we make in this life impact our future.

While Abrahamic faiths see the world as finite, with a start and finish, the Karmic faiths see the world as without beginning (*anadi*) and without end (*ananta*). While Abrahamic faiths subscribe to the doctrine of equality – everyone is equal before

I Am Divine. So Are You.

the eyes of God – Karmic faiths subscribe to the doctrine of diversity – everyone is unique because of the varying karmic burden. While Abrahamic religions actively reject social inequality through acts of charity, Karmic faiths accept social inequality as part of the larger karmic process that humans can only react to with empathy, but cannot actively control. While Abrahamic faiths seek to change society so that it aligns with God's will, Karmic faiths see society as forever changing, cyclically rising and falling. While Abrahamic faiths yearn for salvation, Karmic faiths yearn for liberation from the cycle of rebirths.

Karmic faiths are often confused with tribal and Oriental faiths. The tribal faiths of India are often clubbed together with Hinduism. This is because India does not have a 'uniform civil code'. Tribal communities that do not identify themselves as Christian, Muslim or Parsi, which have their own personal laws, are by default assumed to be Hindu and subject to Hindu personal laws. This has been challenged by secular activists. Oriental faiths such as Taoism, Confucianism and Shinto are often confused with Karmic faiths, and bundled as 'Eastern philosophies', due to the strong influence of Buddhism in East Asia for the past 2,000 years. But none of them have the concept of rebirth at their core.

What Are the Key Features of Karmic Faiths?

Buddhism, Jainism, Sikhism and Hinduism share many common roots.

1. They all believe that the world has no beginning (*anadi*) and the world has no ending (*ananta*). Events happen cyclically.

2. They all believe that nothing happens spontaneously. Every event is an outcome of previous events, including past lives. Events of the past create the present. Events of the present create the future. This is karma.

3. They all believe that humans are blessed because they have the power of the mind that potentially allows them to see the world as it is.

4. The world evokes various sensations, emotions and ideas in the human mind. These can be enjoyed. But we risk beguilement and enchantment (*moha*).

5. Misunderstanding the world, being enchanted by it, trying to control it, letting it control you result in unhappiness.

6. All creatures are trapped in the cycle of birth and death because of delusion (*maya*).

7. Liberation is possible from the material world and the cycle of rebirths, if one is able to see the world as it is and not get enchanted by it.

8. The teachings of wise men and gurus and the practices they prescribe enable us to cope with unhappiness. This may include rituals, prayers, worship, pilgrimage, service, meditation or austerity.

9. *Dharma* is a set of ideas and actions that enables

humans to navigate through this karmic river without getting frightened, and without frightening others. It is rooted in empathy, more than righteousness.

10. *Yoga* is the set of practices that enables us to unravel the mind knotted in fear, spellbound by the world's enchantments.

While Abrahamic faiths place considerable emphasis on 'equality', most Karmic faiths recognise 'diversity' as more important. According to the former, all humans are equal in the eyes of God. In the karmic scriptures, nature is full of myriad creatures – plants, animals and humans, as well as celestial beings – each one a manifestation of a different karmic burden. Their diversity is emphasised over their equal or unequal status. So while Abrahamic faiths focus on homogeneous alignment to God's commandment (one God, one book, one set of rules, one way of life, and equality of all humans), Karmic faiths are highly contextual, thrive in fluidity, and are comfortable with heterogeneity.

To an outsider, this may seem to suggest a condoning of inequality. To the insider, this is a comfort with diversity. The point of Karmic faiths is to show by example how to liberate oneself *from* this diverse, unequal world of accumulating karmic burden.

This liberty *from* the world may appear to contrast modern notions of liberty, which is liberty *to* function as an individual in this world. The quest for liberation is also different from the quest for salvation advocated in Abrahamic faiths. Liberation is about breaking free from karmic burdens, often with the help of a teacher. In contrast, salvation is about being rescued from a world of sin with the help of God's messenger or messiah.

How Do We Distinguish between Individual Karmic Faiths?

Though they all believe in rebirth, hence karma, individual Karmic faiths are very different from each other.

Amongst the Karmic faiths, Hinduism is the least institutionalised and Sikhism is the most. Hinduism has myriad holy books; however, it is not a 'faith of the book' in the manner of Abrahamic faiths. Here, experience generally matters over text. That is why oral discourse of the guru is more important than the written word. By contrast, Sikhism does locate itself in a holy book, the Granth Sahib, which is not so much a set of instructions as it is a set of hymns to be contemplated upon. Buddhism can be traced to one leader, Buddha, who lived 2,500 years ago, and Sikhism can be located to ten gurus, who lived in the past 500 years. The Jain sage Mahavira, who is seen as a contemporary of the Buddha, is not the founder of Jainism but considered the last of twenty-four great teachers (Jinas) of this era. There have been infinite eras before that, each with its own set of twenty-four great gurus. This notion of eternal paths (*sanatana dharma*) forms the foundation of later Buddhism, and of Sikhism.

The primary conflict in Karmic faiths is between the

I Am Divine. So Are You.

world-affirming householder and the world-renouncing hermit: should we engage in an unequal world created by karmic burden, or do we break free from the world itself? The tilt is towards the hermit in Buddhism and Jainism and towards the householder in Sikhism. Hinduism has all sorts of permutations and combinations in the numerous communities that constitute it.

Buddhism does not believe in the idea of God or soul. It values meditation that will help us come to terms with the impermanence of all things, including identity that entraps us in the cycle of rebirth.

Jainism believes in soul, but not God. It values purification through non-violence, so as to liberate the soul from karmic burden and help it rise towards wisdom. The word 'soul' here is translated as '*atman*'. Unlike the Christian soul which gets contaminated and falls from grace, the soul in Karmic religions is forever pure, though its view is obscured by ignorance and pollution.

Sikhism believes in God and soul, but sees the soul as distinct from God. It values devotion and service as the means to earn God's grace and break free from the wheel of rebirths. Sikhism actively believes in the equality of all human beings.

Hinduism believes in God and soul, and sees them as essentially the same thing, the separation resulting from ignorance. It values meditation, purification, devotion, service and ritual worship. While the soul establishes the equality of all living beings, karmic burden establishes heterogeneity of capability and communities (*varna*/*jati*/caste). Having said this, Hinduism also has a thriving corpus of atheistic writings, such as the Carvaka and Mimamsa schools of thought.

	Buddhism	Jainism	Sikhism	Hinduism
Soul	Does not exist	Exists	Exists	Exists (Soul is God)
God	Does not exist	Does not exist	God is without and formless	God is without and within, with form and formless
Existence of third gender	Yes	Yes	No information	Yes
Monastic order (Hermit life)	Superior	Superior	Inferior	Another way
Householder way	Inferior	Inferior	Superior	Another way
Karma	Yes	Yes	Yes	Yes
Dharma	The Buddhist doctrine	The principle of movement	Religion, or the righteous path	Governance that overturns jungle law
Rebirth	Yes	Yes	Yes	Yes
Liberation	Meditation	Austerity	Devotion	Veneration
History	Timeless, oldest identifiable teacher, Sakyamuni Gautama Buddha, lived 2,500 years ago	Timeless, oldest identifiable teacher, Parsva, lived 2,800 years ago	Timeless but organised 500 years ago	Timeless, oldest scripture, Vedas, is 4,000 years old at least

What Is the History of Karmic Faiths?

A brief journey through history will help us get a better sense of these Karmic faiths. For easy understanding, timelines have been simplified and comparison made with events that have shaped Abrahamic faiths. Please note that the ancient history of South Asia is highly politicised and so there are many who challenge the dating and sequence of events listed below.

Five thousand years ago, when Semitic tribes were still in and around the fertile crescent of Mesopotamia and had not yet migrated to ancient Egypt, an urban civilisation thrived in South Asia in the Indus, and the now-dry Saraswati, valleys. Whether the idea of karma prevailed in its highly organised brick cities is open to speculation as the Indus Valley script is yet to be deciphered. The cities of this civilisation ceased to exist following climatic changes and shifting agricultural patterns from around 4,000 years ago. They were not destroyed by invading Aryan armies, a very popular fantasy that was created by 19th century European Orientalists who went on to support the Nazi ideology.

Three thousand years ago, as Semitic tribes gradually established the kingdom of Israel after their exodus out of Egypt, Brahmins were chanting and transmitting Vedic hymns, attached to fire rituals known as *yagna*, along the Gangetic river valleys in a language called Sanskrit. An earlier form of this language (proto-Indo-European) came to India centuries earlier from Eurasia with a people who had tamed the horse. A similar migration took place westward towards Europe, which explains why there are many linguistic similarities between Indian and European languages. It is in the Vedic hymns that we come across the word 'karma' for the first time. In the early texts (Brahmanas), 'karma' refers to ritual action. In later texts (Upanishads), it refers to both action and reaction.

Around 2,500 years ago, in the centuries that witnessed the Babylonian Exile and building of the Second Jewish temple, monasticism rose in India in the form of Buddhism and Jainism. These saw desire as the cause of suffering and karmic burden, shunned the *yagna* rituals, and propagated world-rejecting lifestyles. They spoke of liberation from suffering, ignorance and worldly life, with words like *nirvana*, *kaivalya* and *moksha*. Buddhist monks travelled across South Asia, to Central Asia, South East Asia and East Asia, taking their monastic ideals and karma with them.

The monastic ideal was countered by the rise of a new kind of Hinduism chronicled in Sanskrit texts known as Puranas from around 2,000 years ago. This period saw (and it has been proven now by genetic studies) the rise of a social order called the caste (*jati*) system by which members of the same profession formed guilds and did not share daughters or food. Eventually, these communities became closed, relatively isolated units. A hierarchy emerged based not just on political and economic realities, but also the notion of ritual 'purity', with Brahmins at the top of the pyramid. While this was happening in South Asia, Christianity rose in West Asia, and spread to the Mediterranean region, transforming the pagan and increasingly fragile Roman

Empire into the Holy Roman Empire.

While the Roman Empire faced attacks from Vikings and other barbarian tribes, Buddhism spread from India via merchant ships to South East Asia including Myanmar, Cambodia, Thailand, Indonesia and Malaysia. It also spread along the silk route and other trading routes to Central Asia, Tibet, China and Japan. It mingled and merged with Shintoism in Japan, Confucianism and Taoism in China, with Bon religions of Tibet, and with the local faiths of South East Asia. Many Hindu gods travelled with Buddhism to these regions. It must be kept in mind that in those days this strict division between Buddhism and Hinduism did not exist and they were seen as part of the same continuum of Karmic faiths. Chinese and Sri Lankan monks travelled to India to visit Bodh Gaya, and to Buddhist monasteries and universities, but this stopped after the arrival of Islam.

Islam rose 1,400 years ago and its influence reached India via merchant ships in the south and marauding armies in the north. With its arrival, Hinduism saw the rise of its own monastic orders, which started writing commentaries such as Vedanta on the nature of divinity, and there was an increasing divide between puritanical Brahminism and sensuous temple traditions. They wrote increasingly of one God and one Truth, underlying the diversity of myriad forms, one of the many themes found in the Vedas. God was seen as with form (*saguna*) and without form (*nirguna*). Poet-saints like Mira and Kabir sang of a personal God, devotion to whom reduced karmic burden. This was the Bhakti movement. It paralleled the rise of the Sufi movement that spread from the Middle East to India. Amidst this shift in thinking was born Sikhism over 500 years ago, on the interface between Hinduism and Islam. Like Islam, Sikhism had a holy book and spoke of one formless God, before whom all are equal.

In the age that witnessed the Crusades, the Renaissance and the Reformation in Europe, Buddhism disappeared from much of South Asia except Sri Lanka and the Himalayan regions. Hindu monastic orders became dominant, which saw all things feminine and sensuous as polluting. The female form was associated with the river of materiality (*samsara*) and the male form with culture as well as monastic orders (*dharma*). The queer form (*napunsaka, kliba, pandaka, kinnara*) was seen as lower still, as it did not produce life and simply existed as an object of pleasure tempting non-queers and, worse, as a perennial pleasure-seeking creature. This rejection of the feminine, the queer, the erotic and the sensual was tempered by the use of sensual and queer language in Bhakti and Tantra traditions, but this suffered a mortal blow when the Europeans arrived with the civilising power of 'Victorian values' and their disdain for 'effeminacy'.

Five hundred years ago, the Europeans came by sea to South Asia as traders of finished goods. Following the Industrial Revolution in Europe a few centuries later, they turned into colonisers who sought to make India the source of raw materials. Colonisation destroyed the village economy, and changed the political and economic landscape dramatically. Karmic faiths were studied and organised by European

I Am Divine. So Are You.

Indologists, and Indians became increasingly defensive, seeking to reform Hinduism along Abrahamic lines. The world wars ended colonisation and gave rise to the Indian nation state that saw itself as secular and sought very hard to keep religion out of politics and economics but failed to provide Indians with a common civil code. The new secular Constitution accepted the 'unnatural' status of queer people by adopting the sodomy laws (Section 377 of the Indian Penal Code) of the British Empire.

Over the past few years, Section 377 of the IPC has been overturned by the Delhi High Court, but reinstated by the Supreme Court of India, which is now reconsidering its decision. Simultaneously, the Supreme Court has declared that transgenders are the third gender and need to be given full rights. Extremist right-wing Hindu movements are on the rise and, like extremist religious movements around the world, assume that homophobia and patriarchy are the right moral implications of their religious doctrine. Hinduism, where temples celebrate the marriage of god and goddess, is being increasingly dominated by self-appointed leaders of the faith, who are often male and glorify celibacy. In the West, the media has popularised Hinduism's association with yoga and naked ascetics on the one hand, and the violence of caste on the other, thus earning accusations of Hinduphobia.

How Do Karmic Faiths Look at Nature?

In Biblical traditions, the Book of Genesis begins with the idea that God created the world out of nothing. Multiple interpretations notwithstanding, in this view, there is a Creator who precedes creation. Man, created in the image of God, has been given authority over the rest of creation.

In contrast, Karmic faiths all agree that the world has always existed. There is no beginning or end. Karma is responsible for the transformation of the world. Human life is but one of the many life forms and but one of many transformations.

The 'river of materiality' is the foundation of Karmic faiths. This is most explicitly stated in Jainism, where the world has six essentials (*dravya*): space (*akash*), time (*kala*), matter (*pugdala*), soul (*jiva*), motion (*dharma*) and stillness (*adharma*). Notice that soul here simply refers to that which makes the inanimate animate. Also notice that here *dharma* refers to the natural principle of motion. Here, there is no concept of God, creator or creation.

The Buddha, the enlightened teacher who founded Buddhism, did not bother with concepts such as creator or creation and focused instead on the root cause of suffering. He identified desire as the cause of suffering or dissatisfaction, resulting in continuous entrapment in the world. Desire makes us create categories of things we want or like or do not want or like. Desire makes us create our own sense of identity and, hence, the notion of the 'other'. Desire makes us identify, categorise,

I Am Divine. So Are You.

compare, judge, yearn, possess and fight. Buddha spoke about achieving *nirvana*: blowing out the flame of identity through meditation that makes us aware of our desires and enables us to outgrow the categories they create.

Buddhism did not believe that there was anything permanent in the world. But Jains believed all *dravyas* are permanent. The purpose of life is for the *jiva* to cleanse itself of all pollutants and realise the truth of the world. *Jivas* who do so reside in Siddha-loka. These are the Tirthankaras, or ford-finders, who are not swept away by the river of materiality.

Karmic texts recognise that the world is made of animate creatures and inanimate objects. What distinguishes them is hunger. Plants feed on inanimate objects. Animals feed on animate creatures. Thus the world is made up of that which is eaten (food) and that which eats (eaters). Feeding is violent. It threatens the existence of animate creatures, who therefore reproduce. Thus, from the desire to stay alive comes desire for food, which results in violence, which in turn results in sex. Sex and violence are intimately connected with the survival instinct. From sex and violence comes karma that binds us to the natural world (*prakriti*). In nature, we find the food chain and the pecking order and the natural instinct to be territorial and dominating to ensure food supply. This is *'matsya nyaya'* or 'justice of the fishes', which means the natural way where the mighty feed on the meek.

Humans are the only creatures who are blessed with a mind (*manas*) that enables them to reject the natural *'matsya nyaya'* or the law of the jungle. In fact, the essential truth of humanity is to reverse the natural chain: fear of death, hunger for life, hunger for food, violence, sex, territoriality and domination. This reversal of the natural process is what is achieved through Buddhist meditation and Jain austerities. This is the path of the hermits or *shramana marga* or *nivritti marga*. The inward gaze.

The world of karma is the world of materiality (*samsara*), and the world of materiality is the world of gender, and all Karmic faiths refer to three genders: male, female and queer. The words for queer are many: *napunsaka* and *kliba* in Sanskrit, *pandaka* in Buddhist Pali literature, *pedi* in Tamil Sangam literature, and words like *hijra*, *kinnara* and *kothi* in contemporary times. This third gender has been translated in various ways: from being hermaphrodite to being infertile, impotent, effeminate, transgender or homosexual. Today, we use the word 'queer' for this.

The existence of the queer is explained in Ayurveda, an ancient medical practice originating in the Indian subcontinent, which sees queer realities as physiological and gender as occurring on a fluid spectrum. For instance, it explains that a man is conceived when the white male seed has more power than the red female seed. The queer is born when the white male seed is of equal power as the red female seed. The female is born when the white male seed has less power than the red female seed.

The existence of queer is also explained in texts that deal with *jyotisha*, a traditional astrological practice that maps the stars corresponding to the karmic routes that humans are bound by. In fact, the planet Mercury or 'Budh', one of the nine celestial bodies, is described variously as eunuch, hermaphrodite and transgender – all essentially queer – and visually imagined as sometimes male, sometimes female, riding a composite beast that is neither lion nor elephant.[2]

How Do Karmic Faiths Look at Culture?

Culture (*sanskriti*) is created by domesticating nature (*prakriti*). It is natural for humans to establish cultures. Culture rises and falls over time. In Hindu Puranas, the creation of the world is visualised as the waking up of a sleeping God, Narayana. The world before that exists in a fluid state. The world after that takes form, until it is time to dissolve, for it is time for Narayana to sleep once again. This evolving and dissolving world connected with Narayana's awakening and sleep is not nature, but culture.

The 'world' can mean either nature or culture. And this often leads to confusion in understanding. But it is the Goddess (nature) that is seen as Supreme, or at best an equal and parallel force of God (mind/consciousness/soul). She is the mother as well as daughter. As mother she is nature, wild and untamed, like the forest, the Goddess Kali. As daughter she is culture, demure and domestic, like the field, the Goddess Gauri. It is the relationship with this 'daughter' that helps us understand the attitude of Karmic faiths towards culture. This is best explained in stories from the Hindu Puranas, which are world-affirming, much more than Buddhism and Jainism that are more monastic, hence world-denying.

Hindu Puranas speak of three forms of God: Brahma, Vishnu and Shiva.

- Brahma is the creator, the 'great-grandfather' of all living beings, and culture. He is referred to in Buddhism and Jainism, along with his son Indra, or Sakra, son of the gods or 'devas'. There are no temples built to enshrine him as he is visualised as enchanted by his daughter/ creation/culture, like his many sons. Brahma and his sons are a metaphor for the myriad manifestations of the 'un-enlightened' mind that seeks answers to life's problems through sensual indulgences and material possessions.

- Shiva is the destroyer. He destroys desire (*kama*) as well as death (*yama*) with his third eye. And that makes him very similar to the Buddha and the Tirthankara. In fact, he is visualised as a naked hermit, smeared with ash, seated on remote icy, stony mountains. But the story that makes him popular is the story of how he transforms into a householder by marrying the Goddess Parvati and fathering sons: Ganesha, who bestows abundance, and Kartikeya, who ensures security.

- Vishnu is the preserver, who takes many mortal forms (*avatars*) to teach humanity the principles of *dharma*. While Brahma and his sons are self-absorbed, and Shiva seeks to destroy the very notion of self, Vishnu tempers the notion of self (*jiva*) with concern, responsibility and

I Am Divine. So Are You.

empathy for the other (*para*). *Dharma* is not about rules (*niti*) or tradition (*riti*). As Ram, Vishnu upholds rules, and as Krishna, Vishnu breaks rules in order to establish *dharma*. *Dharma* is about outgrowing the animal desire to dominate and be territorial, a desire born of the survival instinct.

Every human being seeks wealth and power (*artha*) and sensual pleasures (*kama*) and liberation from karmic burdens (*moksha*), but what binds humans to others is *dharma*, that is the cornerstone of relationships. All Hindu rituals – be it the Vedic *yagna* or the Puranic *puja* – is grounded in the idea of nurturing relationships. Both involve inviting the deity into the house, bathing, clothing, feeding and adoring them, before they are asked to offer grace. This 'giving in order to get' shapes the Hindu worldview. It is 'give and get', not 'give and take' or 'take and give'.

A key concept is the idea of debt (*rinn*). When we repay our debt to others (relatives, strangers, the world at large), we are liberated from karmic burden. We repay our debt by being socially responsible. Monasticism without completing social responsibilities like taking care of the family, raising children and looking after elders is frowned upon and seen as escape.

But while Hinduism valued world affirmation over world negation, it also affirmed the caste hierarchy. In its most fundamental form, *dharma* in Hinduism manifests as '*varna-ashrama-dharma*', which means respecting your station in society (*varna*) and your stage of life (*ashrama*). This means you spend all your life following the profession of your father in four stages: first as student, then as householder who takes responsibility for wife, children, parents, siblings and extended community, then as retired folk who teach the next generation and then prepare for the last and final stage of renunciation. Your caste (*jati*) was based on the profession you followed.

The queer is therefore obliged to marry and produce children (*ashrama-dharma*). The only way queers can break free is by creating a caste of their own, the *hijra* community that functions very much like monastic orders (Buddhist *viharas*, Hindu *mathas*) with a leader and followers. But in the *varna/jati* hierarchy, it is far from the mainstream, below all *varnas*, as the only professions available to them are singing, dancing and prostitution, which resulted in their being seen as polluted by the village, and their vilification as 'criminal communities' during British rule. British laws had a hugely negative impact on the *hijra* and other traditional transgender communities.[3]

In pre-modern societies, people who did not fit into their family and caste structures often moved out of the community in two ways.

1. Those who rejected householder responsibilities became *sanyasis* and joined monastic orders.

2. Those who wanted to celebrate their queer sexuality became cross-dressing transgendered people and joined the queer orders such as the *hijras*.

Both claimed divine forces of either a god or a spirit. Both orders, monastic or queer, followed a strict hierarchy, with submission to a leader who was known as guru. Neither was allowed to be part of the family mainstream. Both had to beg for alms and were invited during festivals and special occasions. But while monks achieved 'spiritually pure' status, the *hijras* were feared and seen as contamination. Their best-case scenario was being summoned to ward off the 'evil eye' through their song and dance. The *hijras* have evolved a language of their own based on Hindi and Farsi (the court language of medieval times based on Persian) and they tend to avoid religious association, castrating themselves in the name of a Hindu goddess but also respecting Islamic faith by taking on a Muslim name.[4]

Urbanisation, education and changes in the political and economic environment have transformed the old *dharma* structure based on *varna* and *ashrama*. New professions are being chosen and no one feels obliged to follow the family profession. Young people are choosing to stay single or divorced. The obligation to take care of old parents is now being seen as a choice. The global discourse is based on the 'equality' paradigm, with women and queers asking for equal rights as men. The secular Indian nation state has given some but not all rights to women, and is ambiguous about queers as it gives full rights to transgenders but criminalises 'unnatural' sex.

The threat to tradition by modernity has resulted in the rise of radical religious voices seeking to restore the 'good old' ways. But these old ways are based on imagination rather than facts. They imagine a hetero-normative, affluent Vedic past where there was no such thing as inequality or oppression.

This fantasy land, popular in right-wing circles, especially amongst the Hindu diaspora, denies the existence of all things queer, despite evidence to the contrary in scriptures, stories, song and temple walls.

A Note on the Castes[5] of India

Caste is a South Asian phenomenon, observed not just by Hindus but also by Christians, Muslims, Jains and Buddhists of the region. There are more than 3,000 castes (*jati*) and 25,000 sub-castes in India, which are traditionally and rather superficially mapped to the four-tier caste category system (*varna*) found in the Vedic scriptures.

The key features of the caste system are as follows:

1. Caste is a community identity.

2. Marriage between castes is frowned upon by most people across the caste spectrum. In India, there are less than 5 per cent intercaste marriages.

3. The caste hierarchy is based on purity; some in the lower castes are seen as 'unclean', giving rise to the practice of untouchability. Typically, the 'purer' castes are also the privileged ones, with greater access to wealth, power and agency.

The British had divided India on the basis of religion, creating the two states of India and Pakistan. After Independence, India preferred the linguistic division of its states. But traditionally, all South Asians had been classified on the basis of their *jati*. The Europeans used the word 'caste' for it.

Jati means a community or a kinship group. *Jati* is inherited from one's father and traditionally it determined one's vocation. One had to marry within the *jati*. Inter-*jati* marriage was prohibited, as was sharing a meal with other *jatis*. This ensured *jatis* existed in relative isolation even when they shared the same space in villages. Even when people convert to Islam or Christianity, the *jati* system persists, as it plays a key role in social group formation and hierarchy.

Endogamy, or marriage only among members of the same *jati*, became rigid 2,000 years ago, but the idea that society is composed of several categories of humans has been found in Vedic hymns that are over 3,000 years old. The word used in Vedas is *'varna'* and probably refers to aptitudes, skill, competence or to social hierarchies found in most ancient societies.

The hierarchy between *jatis* was based on economic and political realities, similar to hierarchies seen in most multi-cultural societies. However, there is one idea that makes *jati* a very unique social structure. It is the idea of 'purity', with some *jatis* being seen as 'untouchables' as their vocation involves contact with pollutants like dead bodies, excrement, dirt and other waste matter. This aspect of the *jati* system has brought it great infamy. The 'higher' *jatis* live in the centre of a village, the 'lower' *jatis* live towards the periphery, with 'untouchables' on the outer edges, and the 'tribals' outside the village in the forest.

A hymn from the Rig Veda describes society as an organism whose body parts are made up of four categories (*varna*) of people. Based on this hymn, priests associated with rituals and philosophy of the Veda classified the thousands of *jatis* into four *varnas*, and located themselves in the topmost *varna* of Brahmins. They placed the ruling class and landowning communities in the second *varna* of Kshatriyas. They located the trading communities in the third *varna* of Vaishyas. Everyone else – the service providers – was placed in the *varna* of Shudras. This fourth group eventually split, with the 'untouchables' and 'tribals' being cast out of the four-tiered (*chatur-varna*) system. The various *dharmasutra* texts, composed at the same time as the Ramayana and the Mahabharata, reveal this tendency to reduce the thousands of *jatis* into four *varnas*, with the explicit intention to give privileged position to the Brahmins and the land-controlling *jatis*. It also reinforced the idea of purity and pollution, contributing to the practice of 'untouchability'.

While many sages and philosophers spoke against this social structure, most rulers of the land respected *jati* as it helped legitimise their rule, and it enabled them to collect taxes with relative ease from communities, rather than individuals, who controlled the land (*Kshatriya*) and the markets (*Vaishya*). Many used Brahmins to establish new villages, and collect taxes on their behalf, thus making Brahmins the powerful agents of God and the God-king. Kings who gave importance to Buddhist and Jain monks more than Brahmins were seen as anti-Vedic, even though they did not actually interfere with

I Am Divine. So Are You.

the four-tiered social structure. Muslim rulers, too, in order to ensure stability, used Brahmins as bureaucrats and tax collectors, and so effectively let the four-tiered social model persist. They used the word '*kaum*' or '*kabila*' for *jati*.

When the Portuguese came to India, they used the word 'caste' for *jati*. They saw it as similar to the European system of clans that valued purity of blood. The British eventually documented castes for administrative convenience, and converted this rather fluid social system into a rigid and documented categorisation, even giving castes to people who really had no castes, and giving them a social status in a standardised national hierarchy, ignoring the fact that the hierarchies of the *jati* system functioned locally with numerous regional variations. Based on caste, the British assigned jobs in the military. Based on caste, they divided cities. Later, they switched from caste to religion, ignoring the caste divides in Indian Christians and Indian Muslims, and amplifying the caste divide in Hindus, insisting that caste was an essential condition of all Hindus, based on books such as the *Manusmriti*, which had originally only documented caste as social practice, not recommended or prescribed it.

Hindus who moved to the Caribbean islands as indentured labour in the 19th century, after slavery was abolished in Europe and America, retained their Hindu identity, but not any caste identity, as the socio-economic conditions there did not have need for caste. British administrators did not bother to document the caste of labourers or classify them as such. But in India, where caste was strongly mapped to socio-economic realities, and where British administrators documented caste and made it an essential category while recruiting for the army (only military castes were allowed) and for the bureaucracy (Brahmin and the landed gentry were preferred), caste not only thrived but was institutionalised. The documentation process also created the religion we now call Hinduism.

When India acquired Independence, the government realised that the caste hierarchy reinforced economic and political hierarchies. To create a more egalitarian society, and to facilitate social mobility, the government decided to introduce reservation in education and jobs for members of 'lower' castes and tribes. For better or worse, the government equated caste with class, and saw the 'upper' castes as the haves and the 'lower' castes as the have-nots, a division that is arguably rather simplistic. Further, it introduced a new category of 'backward' castes who were also provided with reservations. This reaffirmation of caste by Indian governments, along with vote-bank politics, has ensured that the *jati* system thrives even today.

More recently, a new two-tier system of classification of *jatis* has emerged, with the privileged *jati* being termed '*savarna*', and the unprivileged *jatis* being termed 'Dalits'. There is a fight for justice and equality. The aim is to annihilate caste completely based on the writings of B.R. Ambedkar. Religious groups such as the Lingayats, reform movements such as Arya Samaj and social groups such as the Rashtriya Swayamsevak Sangh do not support caste. Yet, removing caste consciousness from South Asia continues to be a challenge.

I Am Divine. So Are You.

A Note on the Tribes of India[6]

As per the 2011 census, tribes constitute 8.6 per cent of the Indian population, which is roughly 104 million people. They are scattered across the subcontinent and include, amongst many others, the Abors and Aptanis of Arunachal Pradesh; Badagas of the Niligiri Hills in Tamil Nadu; the Baigas, Gonds, Murias, Dandamis and Kols of Chhattisgarh; Bhils of Rajasthan, Gujarat and Maharashtra; Santhals of Odisha, Bihar and Bengal; Bhots of Himachal Pradesh; Bhotias of the Garhwal and Kumaon regions of Uttarakhand; Chakmas of Tripura; Mundas, Gonds, Oraons, Hos and Kharias of Jharkhand; and Onges and Jarawas of the Andaman and Nicobar islands.

They range from hunter-gatherer communities fully isolated from mainstream society to those who live around the outer edges of mainstream society. Their assimilation with the mainstream has been a point of great political and economic contention.

Each tribe has its own faith system and mythology that is unique to it. They may or may not subscribe to the idea of karma or rebirth. Most follow some kind of belief in animism, with faith in benevolent and malevolent spirits located in sacred mountains, rivers, trees and caves.

Over the centuries, they have been under pressure to assimilate with local Hindu, Buddhist and Muslim populations. In recent times, many have converted to Christianity under the influence of Christian missionaries.[7]

Tribal attitudes towards alternative sexualities have not been well researched or documented. According to one study, conducted by Citizens Foundation, the Ho tribe of Jharkhand was aware and had a comfortable understanding of male homosexual relationships.[8] However, this cannot be regarded as indicative of a pattern among all tribal communities, as there are tribal associations that claim homosexuality does not exist in tribal culture.

How Do Karmic Faiths Look at Scriptures?

Karmic faiths place greater emphasis on ritual practice than scripture or intellectual analysis. They tend to focus on experience (*anubhav*) rather than understanding (*gyana*). For the Buddhist, meditating is more important than reading the discourses of the Buddha. For the Jain, performing austerities is more important than reading the writings of the Jain sages. For the Sikh, doing service (*seva*) and listening to praise of the lord (*simran*) is more important than analysing the writings and the tales of the gurus. For the Hindu, going to the temple, participating in festivals with fasts and feasts, and hearing stories and songs of gods and goddesses are far more critical than analysing the Vedas and the Upanishads.

That being said, in the 21st century, we have given the highest value to textual analysis and assumed that all religions spring forth from a 'book', a phenomenon that's perhaps an outcome of colonialism. Hinduism has always valued the Veda, but while Western academicians look upon this as a book, Hindus have used it in the sense of an idea, communicated through chants, rituals, symbols, stories, songs, architecture and music. Sikhism, in modelling itself along Abrahamic faiths, chose to create a holy book containing the songs of poet-saints, making it a crowd-sourced, though well-edited, holy book. We must keep this in mind when approaching the scriptures of the Karmic faiths.

While Buddhism does have 'rules for monks', scriptures of Karmic faiths have less to do with rules and more to do with ideas related to the architecture of the cosmos and our relationship to it. The general belief is that rules need to be adapted to place (*desha*), time (*kala*) and quality of community (*guna*), for the world is flexible and fluid, going through periods (*yuga*) that keep shifting. The aim of rules is to facilitate community living (*dharma*) rather than making people good. This is very different from the notion of commandments revealed by God through angels and prophets found in Abrahamic faiths.

Owing to its proximity with Islam and Sufism, Sikhism separated the theological (*piri*, from the Persian word '*pir*' for the sage) from the administrative (*miri*, from the Persian word '*emir*' for leader). The holy scriptures are part of the theological world and in them genders are equal, the householder's life is valourised over the hermit's, and there is talk of the soul being genderless; and they contain no comment that is hostile to queers. In the administrative realm, the queer is invisible, with laws neither including nor excluding them. Hostility towards homosexuality in Sikhism is more an outcome of general patriarchy in society and personal prejudices than a requirement that can be traced back to the faith.

Colonial Indologists tried to create a 'Hindu Bible' using various texts such as the Vedas, the Bhagavad Gita, and the *Manusmriti*, and finally settled on the last to create Hindu personal laws in the 19th century. This was a colonial construction based on an obscure Brahmin text, dated to 500 CE, that had no validity in contemporary culture, facilitated by one William Jones. It informed the Indian Penal Code. The laws against homosexuality and transgenders, however, have nothing to do with the scriptures and are based on Victorian laws.

How Do Karmic Faiths Look at the Queer?

The key to understanding Karmic faiths is to look at stories, for it is through stories that the common folk understood their faith.

In Hinduism, we find many stories where God transforms into Goddess, indicating gender fluidity, as also men turning into women and women into men. This reveals a greater comfort with transgender identities. Although there are images of male–male and female–female friendship, one is never sure if this love is platonic, romantic or sexual, leaving them open to interpretations. Also, many queer themes in stories are metaphors used to communicate complex metaphysical ideas

I Am Divine. So Are You.

in narrative form. These are described in greater detail in the chapter on Hinduism.

Hinduism reveals a greater comfort with transgender stories. For example, there are stories that describe Lord Vishnu becoming a damsel and Lord Shiva becoming half a woman. However, homosexuality is not a dominant theme in Hindu mythologies.

In contrast, Greek mythologies are replete with stories of homosexual love, where men love men, and women love women. Apollo falls in love with Hyacinthus, while his sister Artemis drives Callisto away when she lets a man make her pregnant. There are also many descriptions of man–boy love found in Greek tales. So while Greek mythology reveals a comfort with queer sexuality (invisible feelings), Hindu mythology reveals a comfort with queer gender (visible body).

This divide is reflected in modern LGBTIQ politics. The West, influenced by Greek mythology, exhibits greater comfort with the homosexual than with the transgender. Whereas India, influenced by Hindu mythology, reveals greater comfort with the transgender than with the homosexual.

Significantly, no Hindu, Buddhist or Jain scripture has tales like that of Sodom and Gomorrah from the Abrahamic tradition, popularly interpreted as being about divine punishment against queer behaviour.

How Have Karmic Faiths Been Used to Be Hostile to the Queer?

In hermit traditions of the Karmic faiths, sensuality is seen as causing bondage to the sea of materiality and entrapping man in the endless cycle of rebirths. Sex is seen as polluting and only the celibate man (*sanyasi*) and the chaste woman (*sati*) are considered pure and holy. And so an identity based on sexuality draws much criticism. That is why in Vinaya Pitaka,[9] the code of conduct for Buddhist monks, it is explicitly stated that the queer *pandaka* should not be ordained. Rules extend to women who dress like men, or do not behave like women, which we can take to mean lesbians. Jain rejection of homosexuality also stems from its preference for the monastic lifestyle. Anti-queer comments on homosexual behaviour in the *Manusmriti* are more concerned with caste pollution than the sexual act itself. People involved in non-vaginal (*ayoni*) sex are told to perform purification rites, such as bathing with clothes on or fasting. More severe purification is recommended for heterosexual adultery and rape.[10]

Karmic faiths believe that the living owe their life to their ancestors and so have to repay this debt (*pitr-rina*) by marrying and producing children. This is a key rite of passage (*sanskara*). This is a major reason for opposing same-sex relationships, which are seen as essentially sterile and non-procreative. Sikhism states nothing against queer genders or sexuality but values marriage and the householder's life.

I Am Divine. So Are You.

How Can Karmic Faiths Be Used to Affirm the Dignity of the Queer?

The following are ideas based on Karmic faiths that can be used to affirm the dignity of queer people:

1. There is no concept of Judgement Day in any Karmic faith. God is no judge. There is no such thing as eternal damnation for anyone, which includes queer people.

2. Nature/God is infinite (*ananta*). Infinity has no boundaries (*rekha*), no divisions (*khanda*). It is fluid, like a river. It includes the queer. The human mind is finite and limited and so cannot understand everything. We have to accept even that which makes no sense to us, with love for and faith in the infinite.

3. Our body, our personality and our sexuality are outcomes of their karmic burden. They are therefore natural. Wisdom lies in accepting them as such rather than fighting them.

4. Knowledge helps us accommodate the queer in society. Every society has to change its rules as per the needs of geography (*sthana*), history (*kala*) and people (*patra*). In the past, women were seen as inferior to men, Dalits as inferior to Brahmins, and queers as inferior to straight people. But this is considered unacceptable in modern times. We have to change with the times.

5. We have to think in practical terms:
   a. How to include the queer in our family?
   b. Who will take care of the queer when he/she is old?
   c. How will the queer take care of old parents when they grow old?
   d. How will the queer take the family name forward?

6. Problems with the queer are the same problems we face with young men and women who are increasingly choosing career over family, singlehood over marriage, divorce over staying together, and preferring to have only one child. Old religious practices are being abandoned and new ways are emerging as boys and girls marry across religions, languages, castes and communities. This adjustment is no different from adjusting with queer people.

7. Queer people can get married, for marriage is between souls (*atma*) that have no gender. We give too much value to the body (*sharira*) that can be male, female or queer.

8. No matter what our body (male, female, queer), no matter what our social status (rich/poor, educated/uneducated, married/unmarried, business/service), every human being has to cope with loneliness, sense of invalidation, and feelings of frustration and abandonment. This is universal for all creatures. Wisdom lies in helping people cope with this.

9. God is within us (*jiva-atma*) and others (*para-atma*). Through the other (*para-atma*) we can realise the

infinite divine (*param-atma*). Hence the Upanishadic maxims: there is divinity within me (*aham brahmasmi*) and in you as well (*tat tvam asi*). To discover love and appreciation for the world as it is, not the way we want it to be, is wisdom. Discover God – that is wisdom and love – within you by being more generous and accepting of the queer in you and around you.

10. Everything in the eternal faiths (*sanatana dharma*) has a way out (*upaay*), nothing is fixed, provided we have open hearts, expanded minds, and are willing to 'adjust'.

We must take into account that Buddhism, Jainism, Sikhism and Hinduism are not homogeneous. They comprise numerous sects and communities. Yet the overarching and fundamental wisdom that is common to all Karmic faiths makes ample room to accommodate the queer with innovative solutions.

As far as the state and sexuality are concerned, there is confusion. As mentioned earlier, India has deep and historic comfort with transgenders, although they continue to be on the margins of society. Nevertheless, the Prime Minister of India, Narendra Modi, openly advocated transgender rights in August 2016.[11] Indeed, at a grand festival in Ujjain in Madhya Pradesh in June 2016, the government provided transgenders (known locally as *kinnara*) separate toilets. Contrast this with debates on transgender toilets in the United States and the rise of trans-phobic feminists.

Notably, in Abrahamic religions, God is avowedly masculine and so are most of his prominent prophets. There are tales of homoerotic love, like that between David and Jonathan, son of Saul, and the highlight of the discourse on sexuality dwells on the cities of Sodom and Gommorah destroyed by God for their queer and sensual proclivities.

While the third gender is acknowledged, the rest of the queer spectrum continues to be invisibilised. Thus in India, while transgenders enjoy full civic and human rights, homosexual unions continue to be criminalised under 'unnatural sex' laws. This homophobia can be traced to influences of conservative Christian and Islamic frameworks and to Hindu supremacists trying to reframe Hinduism along Abrahamic lines.

Therefore, it is important to emphasise the fundamental liberalism that lies at the core of Karmic faiths and articulate the strains of beliefs that affirm the dignity of queer expressions: Buddhism advocates a deep sense of shared compassion for the queer and encourages a sense of identity that is authentic and liberated from social and illusory constructions. Jainism advocates non-violence and radical scepticism and, as a result, avoids rushing to judgement about queer realities. Sikhism strongly advocates equality among genders and persons. And Hinduism celebrates diversity, which includes the queer in all of its manifestations.

2

Buddhism: Towards Liberation

By Jerry Johnson

With inputs from Vivek Tejuja and Dr Meera Baindur

- Schools of Buddhism

- Buddhist Discomfort with Sex

- On Transgenderism

- Monastic Buddhism and the Queer

- Enabling Comfort with the
  Queer amongst Buddhists

- Buddhism in the West

- A New Informed Engagement

The Buddha, the prince who became the enlightened hermit and established the Buddhist monastic order 2,500 years ago in India. *(Source: Wikimedia Commons)*

Siddhartha Gautama, a prince of the Sakhya clan from Kapilavattu in modern-day Nepal, was born around 485 BCE. This was a time when Vedic Hinduism was being gradually overshadowed by the rise of renouncing non-materialists. According to popular accounts, Gautama lived a sheltered princely life unperturbed by the world outside the palace gates, until one day, soon after marriage, he wandered outside and for the first time encountered death, disease, old age and an ascetic sage. The experience proved to be a pivotal one.

Traumatised by what he saw, Gautama left his wife and newborn son and spent years wandering in the forests, meeting sages and hermits, as a seeker concerned with the existential questions of the human condition: Why do we exist? Why do we suffer? Why do we die? Is this condition inescapable? Soon he came to be known as the 'ascetic Gautama', wandering around forests like the many renouncers of his time.

The peripatetic sages claimed that fasting and renunciation were the ways of gaining wisdom. So the prince stopped eating and drinking until he was too weak to even walk. This is when a woman named Sujata gave him some milk and honey and revived his health. A few days later, after deep meditation under a peepal tree in the eastern part of India, awareness dawned. Siddhartha suddenly 'woke up' in enlightened realisation. He had become the Buddha, which means the one who is aware, awakened, or enlightened.

Meditation revealed to the Buddha that desire – or dissatisfaction – is the root cause of suffering. Desire compels us to compare, crave, yearn, possess and fight. Thus he spoke of renunciation to the point of complete liberation from desire; indeed, rooting the cause of desire within the notion of the self, the Buddha advocated for a complete liberation from the self – a notion that he considered illusory.

> My mind achieved freedom from the binding effects
> of desiring continued becoming, my mind achieved
> freedom from the binding effects of holding on to
> opinionated views, and my mind achieved freedom
> from the binding effects of ignorance.
> (*Vinaya* III 4 – paraphrased)

It is important to note that in Buddhism, there is no creation story. Indeed, the world cannot even be discussed in terms of creation, existence or non-existence. This radical metaphysical view long predates and goes well beyond the claims of modern theories of idealism, dualism or the ontological primacy of consciousness. His insight, formulated into the doctrine of emptiness, was that ontological identities were impossible; the world and our existence were nothing more than a persistent and persuasive illusion; identities could not be brought into existence without asserting a First Cause – an assertion that had to be regarded as arbitrary and inherently contradictory. Thus, all of existence was explained away as an illusion.

Since there is no world, and therefore no beginning and no end, Buddhism moves from a metaphysic of emptiness to an ethic of non-judgement. There is no Judgement Day or ultimate destinies in paradise or hell. Hence, morality, in Buddhism, is not stipulated in the form of edicts or commandments but rather as orientations of personality or functional habits of behaviour that one must seek to imbibe in order to minimise attachments to the world of illusion and live with equanimity.

Moreover, having dispensed with the idea of creation, the Buddha found no use for the concept of Creator either; instead, preferring to diagnose the root cause of suffering, the Buddha said: 'Why bother with who shot the poisoned dart? Focus on how to remove the venom and cure the wound.'[1]

Buddhism evolved over time into a sophisticated philosophical tradition with many schools of thought and sects as it spread across the Indian subcontinent and into South and South East Asia. Early Buddhism had a decidedly 'religious' character to it – with its central focus on salvific liberation from the burden of karma and the recurrence of existence – unlike its contemporary evolutions that have taken on more scholastic or utilitarian purposes in the service of enriching one's life and relationships.

Buddhism can be broadly classified into the early scripture-based school called Theravada Buddhism (or the school of the elders), and the later school that includes an emphasis on collective emancipation called Mahayana Buddhism, which also accepts other authorities and texts. Theravada focuses on the Buddha, the wise sage, while Mahayana introduced the idea of infinite Buddhas existing in multiple realities, including multiple Bodhisattvas, who delay their own liberation until they remove the suffering of all other living creatures.

Mahayana also introduces the Goddess Tara, the embodiment of compassion, into Buddhism.

There is also the Vajrayana school of Buddhism based in the Himalayan regions of Tibet and Bhutan, where ritual plays a key role on the path to enlightenment. However, in Vajrayana, enlightenment is understood not as a linear process resulting from rituals and meditation but as an unexpected and thunderous experience that occurs only if one is a prepared receptacle for it.

Although Buddhism originated in India and spread across the subcontinent under the royal patronage of Emperor Ashoka of the Mauryan Empire, with the arrival of Islam in the region, Buddhism was almost wiped out in Central Asia and India towards the end of the 12th century. However, it continued to spread across East and South East Asia. Theravada Buddhism is now popular in Sri Lanka, Myanmar, Thailand, Cambodia and the rest of South East Asia, while Mahayana Buddhism became popular in China, Mongolia, Japan and South Korea.

Buddhism is part of the Sramana tradition of India that emphasises ascetic or monastic practices, like Jainism and some sects of Hinduism. Therefore, a large number of rules and regulations were laid down by the monks in the monastic tradition for practice, including rules on sexual behaviour and what were seen as 'unnatural' sexual acts – both heterosexual and homosexual. However, this emphasis on monasticism does not indicate that Buddhism is necessarily queer-phobic, as we shall explore in the subsequent sections here. Indeed, in all of the voluminous texts on the doctrine (the *suttas*), we never encounter any general prohibition on homosexuality as such.

Some scholars argue that from the 5th century onwards in India, Mahayana Buddhism evolved to include instances of sexual imagery to convey important metaphysical truths.[2] For instance, sexual symbolism becomes central to many of Vajrayana Buddhism's rituals and Mahayana's metaphysical insights. Specifically, the feminine and the masculine principles are used to convey non-duality or metaphysical monism. The female form is often used to symbolise wisdom, emptiness and the subjectivity of truths, while the male symbolises compassion, form and the illusion of absolute truths.

Given the milieu in which this emerged, it is surmised that Buddhism was being actively shaped by Vedic Hinduism that prevailed in the Indian subcontinent at the time. Various Buddhist schools developed images of male Buddha and Bodhisattva figures represented in sexual union with their female consorts, much like Hindu deities. And, occasionally, practitioners of these forms of Buddhism integrated sexual practices into their rituals. Some scholars have suggested that the introduction of the feminine principle in Buddhism as the Goddess Tara may have come about as a result of the influence of Shaktism – a doctrinal school of Hinduism that focuses worship on the Goddess as the ultimate Godhead.[3]

Schools of Buddhism[4]

	Theravada	Mahayana	Vajrayana
Geographical spread	South and South East Asia (Sri Lanka, Myanmar, Cambodia, Laos, Thailand)	East Asia (Japan, China)	Tibet, Bhutan
Chronology	Early, pre-Mahayana Buddhism (4th century BCE onwards) that continues into modern Buddhism	Emerges around 1st century BCE and continues into modern Buddhism	Post-Mahayana Buddhism, emerges around 7th century, and continues into contemporary Buddhism
Distinguishing philosophy	Desire is the cause of suffering; we yearn for permanence in a world that is eternally ephemeral	Additionally, wisdom must be combined with compassion	Additionally, wisdom strikes without warning like a thunderbolt; we must constantly prepare ourselves
Distinguishing ritual	Meditation	Prayer, meditation	Ritual, prayer, meditation
Distinguishing icon	Buddha alone with specific hand gestures	Bodhisattva with multiple heads and arms, with or without Tara	Bodhisattva and Tara engaged in sexual activity

I Am Divine. So Are You.

Buddhist Discomfort with Sex

Similar to Hinduism, Buddhist acts of virtue are based on the idea of karma. Actions that are to be avoided are called *'akushala'* or not-good. Such actions are motivated by unthinking and uncontrolled submission to passions and emotions, such as anger, attachment or clinging, hatred and seduction. Any desire or action performed with a state of mind that is driven by these can lead to karmic burden. On the other hand, any action that is motivated by non-attachment, benevolence, authenticity and compassionate understanding is *'kushala'* or good.

Given this framework and its celebration of monasticism, early Buddhism looked upon sexual activity more sternly than other faiths. In the *Samyutta-Nikaya*, an account of the Buddha's earliest discourses describes the gratification of the senses as 'low, vulgar and belonging to the ordinary'. He also identifies the craving for sense pleasures (*kama*) as one of the three primary causes of suffering (*dukkha*).

In the *Kama Sutta*,[5] the Buddha says:

> If one, longing for sexual pleasure, achieves it, yes, he's enraptured at heart. The mortal gets what he wants. But if for that person – longing, desiring – the pleasures diminish, he's shattered, as if shot with an arrow…So one, always mindful, should avoid sexual desires. Letting them go, he will cross

over the flood like one who, having bailed out the boat, has reached the far shore.

According to the *Vinaya Pitaka*, a monk named Sudinna submitted to his mother's pleas and had sexual intercourse with his former wife in order to sire a male heir to the family fortune. This incident is said to have led the Buddha to lay down the first rule of monastic disciplinary code prohibiting sexual intercourse: 'Whatever monk should indulge in sexual intercourse is one who is defeated (*parajika*), he is no longer in communion with the monastic order.'[6]

Over time, all kinds of sexual activity, including masturbation, came to be seen as a distracting indulgence of desires attached to this illusory world. Since desire is seen as the root cause of suffering, shunning all desire, including sexual desire, is necessary to reach liberation.

The *Theragatha* (psalms of the elders) has many tales wherein Buddhism is associated with rejection of both marriage as well as heterosexual sex. Atuma left home and was ordained a priest when his mother wanted to find him a bride. Posiya attained awakening when he was disgusted by his wife's sexual advances.[7]

Buddhism was also disinterested in procreation, which was seen as the mechanism by which beings were chained to a constant cycle of rebirths.

One of the five precepts laid out by the Buddha for lay persons states that one should refrain from sexual misconduct. This term is not elaborated beyond this, except to say that a man should not sexually approach a woman who is married or betrothed. Further, the sexual act must not cause harm, it should be consensual, affectionate, loving and it should not break any marriage vow or commitment. It should also not be abusive, such as sex with an under-age person or rape, and this includes forcing your marital partner into having sex.

The monks and nuns, of course, were explicitly instructed to take the vow of celibacy.

At the most, incest is strongly and explicitly condemned as 'wrongful desire' – which includes the unethical desire of a woman having sexual relations with her son, or bestiality.

The 3rd century Hinayana texts indicate that oral and anal sex, whether with a man or a woman, are violations of the third precept laid down by the Buddha regarding inappropriate sexual behaviour. In later scriptural elaborations, inappropriate sexual behaviour was expanded to include using one's hand on inappropriate parts of the body for sexual activity.

In brief, early Buddhism was focused on the soteriological goal of liberation, or *nirvana*, and found little redeeming value in interest in sex.

On Transgenderism

The Buddhist canon does not presume a world of only two genders: male and female. There is reference to many kinds of genders located along the spectrum of male and female, such as the man-like woman (*vepurisika*), the sexually ambiguous (*sambhinna*) and the androgyne (*ubhatovyanjanaka*). This reveals, at the very least, an awareness of the existence of queer people at the time, certainly transgenders, and probably effeminate gays and masculine lesbians.[8]

Ancient Buddhist texts include several stories about transgenderism. For instance, in the *Dhammapada* (5th century) it is recorded that a man named Soreyya transitioned into a woman after becoming entranced by a monk's complexion. Later she married and also bore children.

In the *Lotus Sutra*, an ancient Buddhist text, the eight-year-old daughter of the Naga king transforms herself into a male while imparting the teachings of Buddhist *dharma*. This account of the gender-transitioning teacher has been interpreted by scholars as affirming the idea that a person of any gender can be a bearer of wisdom and enlightenment. According to Daisaku Ikeda, the president of Soka Gakkai International – a global community of Mahayana Buddhists, the *Lotus Sutra* 'teaches that all living beings possess the world of Buddhahood'.[9]

The Pali Tipitaka also mentions different states and types of transgenders – having characteristics of both genders and the man-like-woman and woman-like-man syndrome.

In the Tamil epic, *Manimekhalai*, the heroine shuns all heteronormative relationships, becomes a monk and turns into a man as many teachers do not accept female students. Manimekhalai finally finds a teacher, Aravana Adigal (possibly Nagarjuna, the great Mahayana Buddhist philosopher, who lived in the 3rd century CE), who accepts her as a disciple, even though she is a woman.[10]

In Tibetan Buddhism, the Mahakala Ma Ning – a genderless or transgendered deity – is revered as the defender of the dharma. The 13th century Tibetan monk Gyalwa Yang Gonpa wrote that Ma Ning signified a balanced state between maleness and femaleness, echoing the preference for the 'middle path' advocated in the early teachings of the Buddha.[11]

The Buddha himself has stated that transgenderism is a result of behaviours or karmic seeds (*vasasa*) spread across lives (*abbokinnani*) and is not an innate truth or a moral fault.

Monastic Buddhism and the Queer

In the early monastic texts that emerged after the Buddha, such as the *Vinaya* in 4th century BCE, male monks were explicitly forbidden from having sexual relations with any of the four genders: male, female, hermaphrodites or intersexed, or with transvestites or effeminate men, also known as the *pandakas*.

The exact meaning of the term '*pandaka*' is still contested. Answers vary from their being eunuchs, homosexuals, passive effeminate homosexuals, transgendered males, intersexed or sexless individuals. Some scholars have argued that the term did not refer to men who experience same-sex desire but to impotent men who could not sire children. The opening passage of the second chapter of the *Kathavatthu* in the 'Abhidhamma' section of the Buddhist canon describes *pandakas* as men who are unable to emit semen.[12]

During this time, Buddhism was engaged in propagating and instituting the monastic orders; hence, the Buddha's proscriptions of sexual misconduct among the monastic *sangha* (ordained community) reflected his concern with upholding the public image of the ordained community as virtuous. Social acceptability was vital for the *sangha*, as it could not survive without material support from lay society.[13]

Celibacy and sexual restraint were encouraged even among lay persons. Sexual restraint included masturbation, because it reinforced sexual desire and therefore constant entanglement with the illusory world of the flesh.

Theragatha tells stories of same-sex love between monks but goes on to disapprove of them as a form of attachment. There is the story of Sangha Rakkhita, a monk who lived in the forest with his companion monk. One day he saw a doe whose love for her fawn prevented her from going too far from it; thus, lacking grass and water, the doe and her fawn were famished. Seeing this the monk realised how attachment entraps us from wisdom. He returned home and admonished his companion for harbouring 'wrong thoughts'. Both of them attained awakening as a result.[14]

Amidst all this, the *pandaka* men, who were deemed to be effeminate, promiscuous and self-advertising, were specifically forbidden from entering the monastery. It appears that the condemnation of *pandaka* men was not for their homosexual identity as much as it was due to the fear of them luring other monks into sexual indulgence and disrupting the equanimity of the monastery.[15]

I Am Divine. So Are You.

This assumption that the *pandaka*'s unrestrainable libido was greater than that of heterosexual men is said to have emerged from an account of a monk (who was a *pandaka*) who sought sexual encounters with other monks. All refused except the mahouts and grooms in the elephant stables. As word of the promiscuous activities of the *pandaka* spread in the local communities, the monastic *sangha* fell into disrepute.

The 4th century CE Mahayana Buddhist writers Vasubandhu and Asanga contend that the *pandaka* has no discipline for spiritual practice due to his unrestrained passions. A similar view is also featured in the *Lotus Sutra*, where the ordained community members were advised to stay away from sexually divergent men.[16]

Some texts of the *Adhidharma* also state that a *pandaka* cannot achieve enlightenment in their own lifetime but must wait for rebirth as a heterosexual man or woman.

The 5th century CE Theravadin scholar Buddhaghosa describes *asitta* ('sprayed') *pandakas* as those 'whose sexual burning is assuaged by taking another man's member in his mouth and being sprayed by semen' and *usuya* ('jealous') *pandakas* as those 'whose sexual burning is assuaged by watching other people having sex'. Interestingly, the *Kurundi Atthakatha* – the commentary on the *Vinaya* – permits both these types to be ordained.[17]

Several other Buddhist commentators such as Yashomitra also refer to various types of *pandakas*: the *pandaka*-by-fortnight (*pakka-pandaka*); the *pandaka* by castration (*opakkamika-pandaka*); the *pandaka* who performs oral sex (*asittaka-pandaka*); the impotent *pandaka* (*napunsaka-pandaka*); and the voyeur *pandaka* (*ussuya-pandaka*).

A similar discomfort is revealed in matters related to women who were seen by ancient Buddhist writers as having greater sexual urges than men. Eventually women were ordained as nuns, but were located lower in hierarchy and segregated from the monks so that they could not tempt anyone. Nuns who engaged in sexual intercourse were expelled automatically from the order. The queers and transgendered were firmly kept out of monastic communities.

But the discomfort with women in Buddhism takes upon an even more specific character – one of entrapment with the householder's life – and by extension with the illusions of this world of desire, dissatisfaction and endless rebirths. As Janet Gyatso explains, 'What really made sex with a woman worse than any other kind was its practical upshot: marriage, children, the householder's life; in short, *samsara* [the desire-driven cycle of lifetimes in the material world]'.[18]

Given all this, it is evident that Buddhism looked upon sexual behaviour – including homosexuality – with some disapproval; however, it did not impose severe *legal* punishments against queer sexual practices among non-monastic lay persons. However, few modern Buddhist states or countries with Buddhist populations, such as Sri Lanka and Myanmar, have criminalised homosexuality in their legal systems. Arguably, this may be a vestige of some of their colonial pasts rather than a direct influence of Buddhist philosophy.

In Buddhist Thailand, the epidemic of AIDS in the

1980s brought homosexuality right to the centre of a social crisis and led to the shift in Buddhist attitudes towards homosexuality from one of tolerance to condemnation. In 1989, the Thai monastic *sangha* went on to confirm that gays would be prohibited from being ordained as priests. Since then, however, Thai attitudes towards LGBT individuals have steadily improved, as reflected in their laws. In 2002, the Thai ministry of health publicly declared that homosexuality was no longer to be regarded as a mental illness or disorder. And by 2005, LGBT people were permitted to serve in the Thai armed forces. More progressively, in 2007 the Thai government broadened the definition of a sexual assault or rape victim to include both women and men. The government also prohibited marital rape, with the law stipulating that both women and men can be victims.

Today, the Buddhist nation of Thailand has become among the most accepting communities of LGBT individuals in Asia. A new constitutional panel is looking to further expand protections to transpersons by codifying it into law.

The current Dalai Lama has also been largely supportive of recognising the full human rights of queer individuals regardless of orientation. Nevertheless, he draws a line of distinction between the Buddhist perspective and a secular or societal perspective on queer sexuality. In an interview he gave in 1997,[19] he said: 'Sexual organs were created for reproduction between the male element and the female element – and everything that deviates from that is not acceptable from a Buddhist point of view'. He continued: 'From a Buddhist point of view, men-to-men and women-to-women is generally considered sexual misconduct. From society's point of view, mutually agreeable homosexual relations can be of mutual benefit, enjoyable and harmless.' He cited the Indian Buddhist texts of Vasubandhu, Asanga and Ashvaghosha as his sources concerning what constitutes inappropriate sexual behaviour.

Enabling Comfort with the Queer amongst Buddhists

One of the fundamental premises of Buddhism – at least in its early form – is its assertion of ontological emptiness. All that we perceive as the particular existents in the world – including ourselves as well as the conception of our 'self' – are illusory phenomena empty of any identity.

Hence, in a philosophical system where an illusory self is ultimately generated from ontological emptiness and is caught up in a cycle of births and rebirths, the idea of the physical body, gender, sex and orientation all become transient and illusory features of metaphysical insignificance.

As such, Buddhism observes that it is futile to establish an obsessive or fixated relationship based only upon physical identity or sexual attraction. Yet the role that the body plays in the sexual act is not denied or repressed; it is, in fact, considered perfectly normal to experience the various phenomena of the body and its interaction with the mind.

Therefore, the blurring or transgression of gender boundaries is not likely to become a major heresy or a sin. In such a worldview, sex and gender become complex cultural and metaphysical 'performances' acted out through the physical body – sometimes even as an amusing indulgence – as opposed to existential realities grounded in objective fact.

Some historians of Buddhism have noted that in Japan, from the 13th to the end of the 19th century, Buddhist institutions promoted an open tradition of comfort with homosexuality.[20] These sexually open environments in Buddhist monasteries even inspired a literary genre called *chigo monogatari*, which extolled intimate relationships between elder monks and younger same-sex acolytes. In one tale, a female Bodhisattva Chigo Kannon Engi takes the role of a young male lover of an older monk who is longing for companionship. After a few years, the acolyte dies, leaving the monk alone again and desolate. The female Bodhisattva then appears before the monk and reveals that she and the acolyte were one and the same and goes on deliver a discourse to him on impermanence.[21]

According to some scholars, this tale expresses both Kannon's compassion for the monk's loneliness and understanding of his desire for a male companion. Kannon teaches him about human transience and the futility of earthly pleasures.[22]

The degree to which Buddhism tolerated same-sex sexual activity even among its ordained practitioners is evident from the fact that the 17th century Buddhist scholar Kitamura Kigin was known to advocate homosexuality over heterosexuality for priests in monasteries as a way to avoid the entrapments of householder duties. Another monk, the founder of the Shingon school in Japan, Kooboo Daishi (Kuukai), introduced homosexual acts in his monastery in the early 9th century. Buddhism's disinterest in sexual procreation coupled with a social discourse that saw women as not only inferior to men but also potentially polluting, meant that boys, not women, became the preferred sexual partner. Indeed, these were regarded as the ideal form of relationships. Gradually, this attitude led to the emergence of a curious anomaly in modern Japanese monastic society, where now it is mostly the nuns who live a celibate lifestyle while monks marry and inherit temple properties.[23]

More recent interpretations of Buddhism have sought to reframe sexual activity and identity – especially queer identities – along the lines of authentic self-expression and fullness of being. For instance, in an interview with news journalist Larry King about homosexuality, the Dalai Lama said:[24]

> That's a personal matter. People who have a special tradition, you should follow according to your own tradition...But non-believers, that's up to them. Different form of sex? So long as it's safe, okay! And fully agreed, okay! Bullied? Abused? That's what is wrong. That's a violation of human rights.

What the Dalai Lama does here is contextualise sexual desire within the larger issue of human rights, which align with the core Buddhist values of equality, compassion and loving kindness. It is widely accepted in Buddhism that the monastic life is not a prescription for everyone in general but only for monks who are engaged in serious and exclusively religious pursuits.

The core belief of Buddhism is that one should liberate oneself from a cycle of suffering and in doing so still cause no harm or suffering to others. So bullying others is fundamentally wrong, as it is an act of violence, but love and same-sex desire (with all the safety and cares of any relationship) between consenting human beings is not looked down upon, according to the Dalai Lama.

To demonstrate this point, on the topic of same-sex marriage, the Dalai Lama emphasised:

> That's up to the countries' laws. It's okay, I think it's individual business. If a couple really feels that way, practical, satisfaction…if both sides fully agree, then okay!

Since the karmic beneficiary of one's actions according to Buddhism is one's own self, the Dalai Lama focuses on the matter of same-sex marriage as an issue about consent, conduct and responsibility rather than a matter about the natural order of human sexuality.

Likewise, Hsing Yun, a notable proponent of humanistic

Buddhism in contemporary China, has stated that Buddhism should never teach intolerance towards homosexuality, and that people should expand their minds.

> People often ask me what I think about homosexuality. They wonder, is it right, is it wrong? The answer is, it is neither right nor wrong. It is just something that people do. If people are not harming each other, their private lives are their own business; we should be tolerant of them and not reject them.
>
> However, it will still take some time for the world to fully accept homosexuality. All of us must learn to tolerate the behaviour of others. Just as we hope to expand our minds to include all of the universe, so we should also seek to expand our minds to include all of the many forms of human behaviour.
>
> Tolerance is a form of generosity and it is a form of wisdom. There is nothing anywhere in the Dharma that should ever lead anyone to become intolerant. Our goal as Buddhists is to learn to accept all kinds of people and to help all kinds of people discover the wisdom of the teachings of Shakyamuni Buddha.[25]

The emphasis on expressing one's authentic self, which has now become popular in contemporary Buddhist interpretations and in schools of psychology that rely on

Buddhist principles, borrows its legitimacy from one of the earliest stories about the last words of the Buddha as he lay dying. At the time, the Venerable Anand, his companion, was weeping because the Buddha was leaving the body and he said to the Buddha: 'You are leaving and I have not yet become enlightened. What about me? What will happen to me? The world will be absolutely dark for me – you were the light. And now you are going. Have compassion on us.'

The Buddha opened his eyes and said, *'Appo dipo bhava'* – 'Be a light unto yourself'.

This has come to mean that one's fundamental duty is to be true to one's self and follow the light within us.

Moreover, in the tales of the Jatakas, which is a voluminous body of literature native to India concerning the previous births of Gautama Buddha, there is continuous reference to not just a constantly recurring wife of a Bodhisattva but also to a recurring male friend and companion, usually Ananda.

The two are described as good-looking and childhood friends over lifetimes: sometimes as two deer, sometimes as two humans, sometimes princes, sometimes outcasts. In one story, an old monk Kessava falls ill when his young companion Kappa is called away by the king. Kessava recovers his health only when the king sends Kappa back. The stories convey a sense of congenial camaraderie between the Buddha and his male companion.[26]

Contemporary Buddhism has shifted the emphasis of sexual discourse from that of entrapment in *samsara* (endless rebirth in the world of material illusion) to one of empathetic liberation. In response to the persistence of illusion, the Buddha exhibits empathy for the condition of craving and attachment. His teachings on celibacy arise out of his observation that freedom from desires requires abstaining from indulging those desires.

As a result, Buddhism has now largely come to focus on the shared human condition of dissatisfaction – arising from varied causes including sexual desire – and engenders an empathetic response of understanding rather than condemnation, to gradually progress on the path of self-acceptance and then self-transcendence and, ultimately, to liberation.

Buddhism in the West

Buddhism in the West is highly influenced by Western philosophical roots in secular humanism, individual human rights and critical inquiry. As a result, the Buddhism of the West has a relatively gay-friendlier and secular character than its counterparts in the East.

The Juniper Foundation, which is a Buddhist organisation founded in the West, wrote an article in support of same-sex marriage, stating:

> The heart of Buddhist thought is its insight philosophy, which uses critical inquiry to challenge dogma and to reveal how seemingly fixed ideas are more arbitrary than we might think. Applying this

I Am Divine. So Are You.

philosophy, we see that social customs are not fixed laws but evolving conventions that serve a purpose in a particular culture and time. Marriage is one of these conventions. It is not a rigid law but a social custom that evolves.

As Jeff Wilson observes: 'Buddhist same-sex marriage was born in the USA…as an act of love, not activism.'[27] In the United States, the Buddhist Churches of America, representing Jodo Shinshu Buddhism, which is the largest school of contemporary Buddhism in Japan, were among the first to conduct same-sex marriages. The Rev'd Koshin Ogui of the Buddhist Church of San Francisco performed the first recorded Buddhist same-sex marriage ceremony in 1970, even before the gay rights movement gained prominence. In the years that followed, other Jodo Shinshu priests followed suit. These marriages were performed as acts of compassion and loving kindness – central character traits that a Buddhist must nurture.[28]

By the 1990s several Jodo Shinshu ministers were performing same-sex weddings. In April 2000, the Rev'd Masao Kodani of Senshin Buddhist Temple in Los Angeles was asked to marry two women, one of whom was a male-to-female transsexual. The Rev'd Kodani approached the highest doctrinal experts of the head Jodo Shinshu temple in Kyoto to ascertain whether this was a problem. The doctrinal experts responded that there was no problem, as long as the couple was sincere.[29]

Likewise, the US Branch of Soka Gakkai International

(SGI), a Japan-based religious movement influenced by Nichiren Buddhism, announced in 1995 that they would also conduct wedding ceremonies for same-sex couples. Nichiren Buddhism, which is a branch of Mahayana Buddhism based on the teachings of the 13th century Japanese monk Nichiren (1222–82), is generally noted for its belief that all people have an innate Buddha nature and are therefore inherently capable of attaining enlightenment in their current form and present lifetime.

SGI President Daisaku Ikeda said: 'Buddhism upholds equality and expounds supreme humanism. All human beings have equal rights. There is no difference whatsoever in their inherent dignity. So, no matter what you may face, please live with pride, confidence and courage.'

Various Buddhist organisations founded in the West are now voicing their support for same-sex marriage and its legalisation. In fact, several LGBT people have also been ordained as Buddhist monks or clergy in these Western organisations.

A New Informed Engagement

According to the Buddha, it is individual free will or intentions rather than fate or circumstance that drives karmic action. While one cannot change the world and what is given to us, we can focus on changing our actions and intentions to help us move towards liberation from suffering.

But to act with wisdom, one will have to come to terms with the fundamental truths of reality: namely, that everything is impermanent or transient; *dukkha* (suffering or dissatisfaction) arises because of desires; the self is illusory; and emptiness is ontological.

The four truths express the basic philosophical orientation of Buddhism:

1. Humans crave and cling to impermanent states and things, which leads to *dukkha* or dissatisfaction and suffering.

2. This craving and clinging produces karma which leads to renewed becoming, keeping us trapped in rebirth and renewed dissatisfaction in an endless cycle of repeated rebirths of desire and *dukkha*.

3. Cessation of desire is the only way to stop earning karmic burden and end this cycle of rebirths.

4. Following the Eightfold Path is the way to liberation or *nirvana*.

By following the Noble Eightfold Path, restraining oneself, cultivating discipline and practising mindfulness and meditation, craving and clinging will be stopped, and rebirth and dissatisfaction are ended.

In ancient Buddhist texts, we find that four sublime states of mind are identified by the Buddha: love or loving kindness (*metta*), compassion (*karuna*), empathetic joy (*mudita*), and equanimity (*upekkha*). These states of the mind, called

Brahma-viharas, are values we must adopt when we interact with others in the world. While these values would be great for any person to follow, in the context of a queer person's orientation in a heteronormative world, these values of the mind take on special significance and psychological power.

The combination of a philosophical framework of impermanence with a psychological orientation of mindful compassion, Buddhism empowers one with formidable mental-health resources to negotiate any situation of conflict or struggle that one would encounter in the world, especially as a queer minority.

Nyanaponika Thera writes about these mental states: 'They level social barriers, build harmonious communities, awaken slumbering magnanimity long forgotten, revive joy and hope long abandoned, and promote human brotherhood against the forces of egotism.' The *Digha Nikaya* 13 discusses these mental attitudes and their cultivation in detail.

It may seem difficult to cultivate *'metta'* or loving kindness in the face of a world that may be at best indifferent to queer struggles or at worst an active contributor. It is instinctual to react with anger, humiliation or aggression. However, the Buddhist way would be to remind ourselves about *akushal* actions in a world of an illusory self: Where is the self that is being humiliated? Is the humiliation real? Have we affirmed our self as metaphysically real when it is not? Can the self be attacked when it does not even exist? Attachment to this illusory self is the cause of our own suffering, Buddhism would observe. To believe that our emotions arise in reaction to another person's actions against us is to grant metaphysical objectivity to emotions and, by extension, to the self and the world.

According to the Thich Nhat Hanh, anger blocks dialogue and fruitful communication. 'The surest way to change this is by carefully attending to the stories of each other's lives through one-to-one dialogue,' says SGI President Ikeda.

Therefore, an informed engagement with this world, according to Buddhism, would require that we adopt a balanced middle path between complete attachment and complete detachment. Complete attachment would trap us in the cycle of dissatisfaction and suffering; complete detachment would deny us the ability to imbibe *metta* and *karuna* for others who, like us, are also trapped in the world of the illusory.

The middle path allows us to engage with others from a place of compassion and equanimity. It allows us heightened awareness of our emotional responses.

William Edelglass relates Thich Nhat Hanh's fourteen mindfulness trainings, one of which is excerpted below:

> Only love and understanding can help people change...If I was born a pirate and raised as a pirate, I would be a pirate now. Each shares the responsibility for the presence of the pirates... The eyes of compassion are also the eyes of understanding. Compassion is the sweet water that springs forth from the source of understanding. To practise looking deeply is the basic medicine for anger and hatred.[30]

In the *Karaniya Metta Sutta*,[31] the Buddha says:

> Let none deceive another or despise any being in any state. Let none through anger or ill-will wish harm upon another. Even as a mother protects with her life her child, her only child, so with a boundless heart should one cherish all living beings, radiating kindness over the entire world, spreading upwards to the skies, and downwards to the depths, outwards and unbounded, freed from hatred and ill-will. Whether standing or walking, seated or lying down free from drowsiness, one should sustain this recollection. This is said to be the sublime abiding. By not holding to fixed views, the pure-hearted one, having clarity of vision, being freed from all sense desires, is not born again into this world.

The *Sutta* exhibits an attitude that shows intentionality and the practice of being deeply aware of oneself and one's mental states. There are these insights in this *Sutta* that we can take away:

1. Wish no ill or harm upon anyone.

2. We must strive to extend our loving compassion to all beings – LGBTQ persons, the homophobe, the bigot or the saint.

3. We must be mindful of our emotional states and practise the awareness of being kind at all times.

4. We must not be attached to our own point of view, for this may cloud our practice of kindness and empathy.

In this way, Buddhism suggests a novel approach to engaging with each other in the world. Its recognition of the universality of suffering in which we are all trapped animates the need to be kind and compassionate. Being kind to one another will create the necessary psychological framework for mutual understanding and the cessation of dissatisfaction.

Buddhism observes that we are not kind because we listen, we are kind and therefore we listen. When we truly understand that suffering permeates this world, we will be able to wipe it out with kindness and equanimity.

So while one of the first documented anti-queer proscriptions is found in early Buddhist scriptures, we also see the earliest recorded same-sex marriage in modern society being conducted by a Buddhist organisation in the US.

This interpretation of Buddhism allows an individual – queer or otherwise – to blossom into the fullness of their compassionate self, mindful of their nature as not merely the body or gender or orientation. It is a worldview that does not choose to withdraw into ascetic indifference to the suffering of others but one that engages deeply, empathetically and lovingly with their own condition and that of others around them.

3

Jainism: A Quest for Non-violence

By Jerry Johnson
With inputs from Sachin Jain

Parshva, the 23rd Tirthankara, or Jina, of the current human era, according to Jain traditions, is identified by the hooded serpent under whose shade he stands. Jain monks rejected the idea of wearing clothing and firmly believed in non-violence. Jains saw all sexual desire, heterosexual or homosexual, as fetters to the material world. *(Source: Wikimedia Commons)*

J ainism is the religion of the Jina, which literally means 'conqueror'. This is, however, not a reference to the conqueror of worlds but of inner landscapes of the mind and character. A Jina attains victory over his own anger, pride, deceit, desires and greed.

From Jainism comes the concept of non-violence (*ahimsa*): it is not just about not hurting the physical body, it is also about not hurting another's self-identity, expressed through a point of view, or behaviour. Only when one is truly non-violent in this radical sense is one liberated from the karmic river of materiality.

A Brief History

Jainism originated in India at around the same time as Buddhism. It is said to have been established by Vardhamana, later called Mahavira – or the great winner – in about 500 BC.[1]

Jains believe that everything is imbued with life and (detectable and undetectable) consciousness, including things such as stones, trees, plants and mountains. As a result, the concept of non-violence against all living beings is central to Jainism. Practising Jains are vegetarians and they avoid eating the roots of plants.

The Jains believe the world is timeless and there is no 'creator'. The world has always been around and will always be governed by the laws of karma. Like in Buddhism, there is no concept of Judgement Day in Jainism. With the passage of time, things go from better (*sushama*) to worse (*dushama*) and back again to being better. This recursive process of ascending and descending epochs occurs with unfailing regularity for eternity.

As the souls of living beings move through these recursive epochs, they gather karmic burdens that pull them down to the lower realms of suffering, much like a floating balloon weighed down by rocks. Through austerity and non-violence, one can reduce the karmic burden and rise up towards higher realms. The highest realm, according to Jainism, is Siddha-loka, inhabited by the twenty-four sages known as Tirthankaras, who have attained *kaivalya* or full knowledge of the universe. They have purified their souls from all karmic burden and hence will never be reborn.

Of all the beings in the world, only twenty-four achieve this state in every epoch, and there have been and will be endless such epochs for eternity, each with its own twenty-four supreme sages. Mahavira, symbolised by the lion, is the last Tirthankara of our era.

In the post-Buddhist period, Jainism spread south to Karnataka and Tamil Nadu, as indicated by the presence of many Jain caves in the region. The religion was patronised by many kings such as Kharavela of Odisha 2,100 years ago and Pulakesin Chalukya of Karnataka 1,400 years ago before being completely overshadowed by Hinduism. While Buddhism disappeared from the Indian subcontinent, Jainism managed to survive perhaps because its emphasis on non-violence led most Jains to pick professions in banking, trading and business, which led to their deep integration with the economic life of mainstream society.

Today, the most dominant Jain communities reside in the states of Gujarat and Rajasthan, though there are significant numbers in other parts of India, such as the Gangetic plains, Karnataka and Tamil Nadu.

Jains have two major groups:

- The more austere Digambara, whose male monks do not wear any clothes, and

- The Shwetambaras, whose monks and nuns wear white robes.

As mentioned above, Jain followers have over centuries adapted to banking and trading activities instead of farming or animal husbandry. They became renowned as moneylenders, not discriminating between Hindu kings, Muslim sultans, or even the East India Company. As a community, Jains continue to dominate India's business and entrepreneurial sectors.

Philosophy

Jainism believes in a naturalistic universe: all that exists is real. This metaphysic stands in contrast to that of Buddhism, where the existence of the universe is considered an illusory phenomenon, or *'maya'*. Both matter and spirit – or consciousness – are real and eternal. There are an infinite number of souls and objects in existence and all are real, not mere phenomena. They may change forms over time but remain in real existence forever.

The conscious entities are called '*jiva*' and the non-conscious entities are called '*a-jiva*'. The former entities go through life accumulating karmic burden – which is a consequence of either meritorious actions or demeritorious actions. So the purpose of a conscious entity's life is to minimise its karmic burden over time in order to attain *moksha*, or liberation, of the soul.

A core principle of Jainism is the experience of unity with all living beings. The word '*sangha*' – which means a collective or communion of monks, nuns and lay votaries of the Jain community – also connotes the idea of equality of all people irrespective of caste, creed, sex, status or race. This principle of equality and communion with all living beings animates the very central practice of Jainism, which is radical non-violence. As a Jain sage put it: 'The way I don't like sorrow, other beings also do not like it. Therefore, I avoid violence, ask others to avoid the same, and do not inspire violence in others.'[2]

When a Jain calls himself a '*shramana*' he believes that he takes ownership and responsibility for his own self-development or decadence, his own happiness and sorrow, growth and decline. Therefore, he is committed to a sincere effort of self-excellence. This can be accomplished by becoming self-reliant and self-exerting. Similarly, a '*samana*' acts to extinguish or quieten down his inner landscapes. For instance, he consistently calms his own emotional outbursts and controls his anger. Thus, a Jain monk practises in equal measure *shramana* and *samana*, self-excellence and

I Am Divine. So Are You.

arduousness as well as self-control and calm, in order to achieve equanimity and communion with all living beings.

To explore what Jainism has to say about sexuality and gender, let us first explore its ethical framework. Jainism is an atheistic religion, in that it does not believe in a Creation metaphysic. Therefore, its ethical dimensions are brought about through observances of natural and social interactions rather than divine revelation. Enormous collections of Jain literary expositions deal with discipline, observances and ethical conduct. For example, the *Mulachar* of Vattakera and the *Dusvaikalika Sutra* are scriptures that deal with right conduct.

Conduct

Jainism celebrates the monastic lifestyle. As such, the Jain monk is considered an exemplar of virtuous Jain living. However, laypersons are equally encouraged to follow the principles of a monk's life as much as possible in order to live the good life.

A monk takes five great vows before being ordained:

1. Non-violence

2. Truth

3. Non-stealing

4. Non-possessiveness

5. Chastity

In addition, a monk is expected to be mindful about his practice of radical non-violence in the way he walks, speaks, eats or answers the call of nature. This is to ensure that his acts are as minimally violent to other living beings to the fullest extent possible to him.

While these practices are recommended to a lesser degree to laypersons, the ordinance to be vegetarian, non-violent, and to avoid any deceit, fraud or emotional indulgence applies in equal measure.

Jains believe that a layperson (*shravaka*) can earn spiritual merit by taking care of the monastic order (*shramana*). They are strict vegetarians, who shun root vegetables and eating after dark. A key part of Jain living is austerity, displayed in practices such as observing regular cycles of fasting and celibacy.

In essence, Jainism is oriented towards the inner life of the soul and every concomitant practice that can liberate the soul from the karmic burden of actions performed by the body. Thus, its focus on right conduct is merely instrumental in the primary purpose of attaining *moksha*. The body is at best the instrument through which karmic burden can be reduced; at worst, the body is the cause and source of karmic pollution.

Therefore, in order to tread towards spiritual evolution and realisation, Jainism emphasises the importance of renunciation, self-abnegation and meditation along with the purification of the soul. A Jain is also encouraged to develop the capacity for self-concentration or mindfulness. This will eventually lead one to discard the identification of the self with one's body or temporal relationships and realise the unity

I Am Divine. So Are You.

of the universal living energy.

This is the realisation that the greatest seers of the Jain tradition have been able to grasp and imbibe. For Jains, the observance of a religious life is the means through which equanimity and perfect unity with the universe become possible. In a poetic sense, the Jain ideal is for the soul to submerge within the perfect stillness of the universe.

Matters Related to Sex

Given the central focus on the immaterial soul over the impermanent body, one could easily surmise that Jainism would not look too kindly upon the indulgence or celebration of the body through sexuality and orientation. Moreover, to assert one's gender identity or fluidity would be seen as a fallacious and foolish focus on the transient, the temporal and, ultimately, the metaphysically unimportant. Indeed, Jainism regards that these distractions ensure that *moksha* becomes unattainable and the soul remains trapped in wandering through the infinite cycles of death and rebirth.

So, while Jainism has nothing specific to say about homosexuality or queer expressions in particular, its silence on the topic cannot be construed as either endorsement or condemnation. All sexuality is problematic for Jainism, even heterosexuality. Sex for the purpose of procreation within a marriage is tolerated in the recognition that a monastic life may not be suitable for everyone at all times or in their current birth. Therefore, procreative sex can be seen positively as contributing potential future practitioners of Jainism.

Thus, Jainism reacts the same way to homosexuality as it would to non-procreative heterosexual acts of sex – as an indulgence of the body and a submission to one's emotional outbursts that disturb equanimity and keep one preoccupied with the material world.

Matters Related to Gender

Ancient Jain scriptures acknowledge three genders of the physical body – the masculine, feminine and the neuter. The *Tattvaartha Sutra* explains these and their accompanying sexual characteristics in great detail. It goes on to describe the external physical signs of these characteristics as well as their internal motivations of desire. One can understand this in modern terms as acknowledging the difference between physiological sex, psychosocial gender, and sexual attraction or orientation.

In Chapter 2 of *Tattvaartha Sutra*, aphorisms 50 and 51 reveal the Jain attitude towards gender as they describe three worlds:

1. The upper world of heavenly beings who display either male or female characteristics.

2. The lower world of hellish beings who are neuter gendered and have mixed sexual characteristics.

3. The middle world of humans and animals, who may be male, female or neuter.

Further, it asserts that the gender possessed is a consequence of karmic actions from previous births, but the sexual characteristics and desires are a consequence of mental unease. This is found to the least degree in the male gender and progressively increases in the female and neuter genders.

Although Jains have monastic orders for women, the traditions differ on the issue of female enlightenment. The Digambara Jains believe that women are capable of spiritual enlightenment, but not in their current physical form; their souls must be reborn in a male body in order to attain spiritual liberation. This may perhaps explain why all the twenty-four Jain Tirthankaras – or the grand sages worshipped by Jains – are men.

In contrast, the Shwetambara Jains maintain that liberation is attainable by both men and women in their current forms. The relevant factor is not the gender but the agency of free will that comes only with a human form.

In Shwetambara lore, the 19th Tirthankara Malli-natha was born with a woman's body (not so in Digambara lore) as a consequence of duping his friends in a previous lifetime, by performing more austerities than they did to reduce his karmic burdens. Hence, although he became a Jain Tirthankara and is regarded as male, his name – which translates to Lord Jasmine – and his symbol of a pot both allude to his femininity.

Enabling Comfort with the Queer amongst Jains

While it may appear that the Jain antipathy to the material world and specifically to the physical body would make it insurmountable to reach common ground with queer acceptance, Jainism includes within its corpus of ideas a core principle to achieve precisely this goal.

One fundamental principle of Jain thought is *'anekantavad'* – or epistemological subjectivity (can also be translated as epistemological multiplicity). Jainism holds this principle as central to understanding the world. The truth of anything can be concluded – if at all – only after considering all aspects in context and relevance. Even then, the subjective perception of truths plays a role in one's apprehension of them. Hence, anything explored through a multiplicity of subjective views yields even more information and truths. Acknowledging this is not necessarily incompatible with an objective metaphysical reality. According to Jainism, facts exist external to the perceiver, who may use a multiplicity of modes to apprehend them.

Indeed, Jainism also leads to radical epistemological scepticism that arises from this subjectivity, since it argues that no one person can apprehend the totality of all truths in an infinite universe. This lends itself well to acknowledging the plethora of diversity and hitherto unknown expressions of identity or sexuality among humans, celestial beings, and living species within this universe.

Epistemological scepticism also emerges in alignment

with the Jain practices of radical non-violence in action and equanimity in attitude. Without a sense of entitlement or ownership over the truth, Jains can navigate conflicting points of views with ease, calm and humility. Thus, the idea of judgement, condemnation or punishment are eschewed in favour of accommodation and acceptance.

Aiding this application of the principle of *anekantavad* is the doctrine of *naya*, which looks for the common essence among views that may appear disparate or even contradictory. The *naya* doctrine asserts that the seeming differences in objects, views and truths perhaps arise from the specific aspects of the objects one happens to fix one's attention on. We sometimes trust our cognitive operations but this may be incomplete in its coverage of objective reality. Our perceptions may also be obscured by egoism or conceit or biases, which may cause us to have partial apprehension.

Here, human consciousness necessarily imposes a filter or framework on perception, thereby actively adding elements to that which is being perceived and determining the form, mode and manner of our perception. In other words, consciousness is an active contributor to the perception of reality and not a passive observer or receptacle of reality.

In Jain treatises, these principles address the relationship of the soul with karmas and the implications thereof for *moksha*. In order to arrive at deeper truths beyond the reach of the senses, Jainism cautions us to eschew self-centredness and encourages us to appreciate the best in others. In the context of queer lives, the principles of *anekantavad* and *naya* can offer one a perspective on diversity, sexuality and human variations that may be overwhelmingly too complex to be grasped by one's current faculties and conceptual abilities. In the face of this complexity, the Jain's response would be acceptance of these alternative queer realities at best or tolerance of them at worst. The individual is recognised as autonomous and free to decide the destiny of one's soul and karmic burden as one sees fit.

With regard to the position of women in Jainism, there is little evidence to support any egalitarian view of the genders in Jain scripture. Having said that, in some local traditions of Jainism, such as in the Shwetambara tradition, the demi-goddess Padmavati is worshipped, although not quite at the stature of the grand ascetics such as the Tirthankaras. Padmavati is sought after by those who seek material pleasures in this life, hoping to eventually outgrow their karmic hunger for wealth and power and fame, and thereby be able to walk the path of the Jina. Though her name associates her with a lotus and hence with Lakshmi, she is also a fighter and guardian goddess like Durga in Hinduism, who along with her husband, Dharendra (Indra of the earth), protects Parshva, the 23rd supreme sage of this era.

A New Informed Engagement

The synthesis of *anekantavad* and *naya* allows us to adopt multiple standpoints from which to look at the world. Take, for instance, the concept of the soul. In a certain sense, the soul is one – an eternal, continuous, immaterial and unbound entity. From another perspective, the soul is multiple in number – as many as there are living beings in the universe. In a certain sense, the soul is changing forms, fleeting across species and lifetimes. It may be immaterial in terms of matter, but is real in terms of its own substance. In one sense the soul is unbound and liberated but in another sense it is also bound to karmic causality.

In the context of social interactions, these principles allow us to find pluralism in unity and permanence in the presence of change. Since Jains know that differences exist but the underlying reality of the universe is common, we can acknowledge the multiplicity of viewpoints with a deeper sense of empathy for the other's perceptions and a sense of humility in the limitations of our own.

Therefore, in contrast to the principles of non-contradiction and the excluded middle from Greek philosophy, Jain logicians have formalised a sevenfold predication of assertions about knowledge as follows:

1. From a point of view, something 'is'.

2. From a point of view, something 'is not'.

3. From a point of view, something 'is' and 'is not'.

4. From a point of view, something is 'indeterminate/ inexpressible'.

5. From a point of view, something 'is' and is 'indeterminate/inexpressible'.

6. From a point of view, something 'is not' and is 'indeterminate/inexpressible'.

7. From a point of view, something 'is', 'is not' and is 'indeterminate/inexpressible'.

Unlike Greek logic, Jains did not regard things as either absolutely existent or non-existent. Judgements are relative – true under certain contextual or meta-conditions and not absolute – and they must be expressed by indicating their conditional or meta-conditional character. Thus the concepts of 'pure identity' – whether of race, religion or sexual orientation – are dismissed summarily because they deny plurality. Objects, having infinite qualities, modes of expression, forms and relations to other things, are neither exclusively particular nor exclusively universal. They are a combination of both, with their identity embedded in difference and similarity.

This epistemology consistently feeds into an ethical framework that holds non-violence as a central virtue of conduct. Since epistemological humility would require one to consider the possibility of truth in opposing viewpoints, the possibility of violence, conflict or repression is eliminated.

In Conclusion

While Jainism has little to say about homosexuality or queer identities explicitly, it proscribes indulgence in physical passions for homosexual and heterosexual individuals alike. This is because Jainism prefers to direct its attention away from the material and the temporal in favour of the permanent and spiritual in search of *moksha*. It does this by advocating radical non-violence and equanimity among living beings, regardless of identity, race, species, sexuality and religion.

Thus, in a radical sense, the posture of non-violence upheld by Jain epistemology parallels its metaphysical emphasis: scepticism and intellectual humility are favoured over claims of certainty and authority, the former being features of the permanent soul and the latter those of a temporal body. It is this feature of Jain philosophy that lends itself to being more accepting or tolerant of diversity, multiplicity and queer realities.

4

Sikhism: All Humans Are Created Equal

By Sukhdeep Singh

- About Guru Nanak

- Guru Gobind Singh and Foundation of the Khalsa

- Key Tenets of Sikhism

- Gender Equality in Sikhism

- Halemi Raj: The Sikh View of Governance

- Sikhism on Transgender Issues

- Coming Out in the Sikh Context

- Marriages in Sikhism

- Modern Sikh Responses to the Queer

- Sikh Religion and Punjabi Culture

- Conclusion: A Probable Way Forward

Image of Guru Nanak speaking to Sheikh Saraf, a cross-dressing Sufi Pir, in Baghdad. *(Source:* B40 Janamsakhi *– an oral history narrating tales from Guru Nanak's life composed many years after his time.)*

Sikhism is one of the youngest religions in India, founded by Guru Nanak Dev during the fifteenth century, which was a period of great political turmoil across the subcontinent. The Mughal invasion from Central Asia into South Asia was decisively transformative. In this context, Hinduism, the religion of the indigenous people of the subcontinent, and Islam, the religion of the invaders, clashed substantively. It was amid such turmoil that Sikhism was born.

The theological body of Sikhism comprises the teachings, hymns and ruminations of ten Gurus (including Guru Nanak). The works of seven of the Sikh Gurus – Guru Nanak, Guru Angad, Guru Amar Das, Guru Ram Das, Guru Arjan, Guru Teg Bahadur and Guru Gobind Singh – as well as the hymns of various poets and Hindu and Muslim saints of the time were compiled into one holy book by the 10th Sikh Guru – Guru Gobind Singh. This book is called the Guru Granth Sahib.

Guru Gobind Singh ordained Sikhs to follow the Guru Granth Sahib as their spiritual teacher, thus bringing an end to the tradition of following a living Sikh Guru. Therefore, the Guru Granth Sahib is considered the 11th Guru of the Sikhs.

Sikhism is unique among Indian religions in that it is monotheistic. *Ek Omkar*, meaning 'God is one', is central to the Sikh doctrine. The Sikh God is formless, ageless and without hate or enmity. The *Mool Mantar* (Main Chant) is the first composition to appear in the Guru Granth Sahib and describes God as:

Ikoa'nkār sa̱t nām kaṟtā purak̲h̲ nirbh̲ao nirvair
akāl mūra̱t ajūnī saibh̲a'n gur parsā̱d

One universal creator God. The name is truth.
Creative being personified. No fear. No hatred.
Image of the undying, beyond birth, self-existent.
By guru's grace.[1]

About Guru Nanak

Guru Nanak, the founder of Sikhism, was born in 1469 in
the village of Talwandi (now Nankana Sahib) in present-day
Pakistan. His parents, Mehta Kalu and Mata Tripti Dev, were
Hindu and belonged to the Kshatriya caste.[2]

From an early age, Nanak had an inquiring mind and
questioned the ritualistic emphasis of Hinduism. At the age
of nine, when his father Mehta Kalu called upon a priest to
conduct the sacred thread ceremony according to Hindu rituals,
Nanak refused to wear the *janeu*. He argued that the ritual
was discriminatory against lower-caste people, and women
were forbidden from wearing the sacred thread.[3] Moreover,
he observed that upon death, the thread burns along with the
body and would serve him no purpose in the afterlife. The
young boy posited that chanting the Lord's Praise is the only
true sacred thread that never breaks and does not wear out in
the court of the Lord.

I Am Divine. So Are You.

Nā-e mani-ai paṯ ūpjai sālāhī sach sūṯ
Believing in the Name, honor is obtained.
The Lord's Praise is the true sacred thread.

Dargėh anḏar pā-ī-ai ṯag na ṯūtas pūṯ.
Such a sacred thread is worn in the Court of the
Lord; it shall never break.[2,3]

– Asa di Var (Guru Granth Sahib, p. 471)

Similarly, throughout his life Guru Nanak spoke against rituals and focused instead on meditating about the nature of God. Once, at the age of twenty-eight, Guru Nanak went to bathe in a nearby river. However, he did not emerge for days and no trace of him could be found. After three days, he returned to his home having attained enlightenment, and proclaimed: '*Na koi Hindu na Muslaman* (No one is Hindu or Muslim),' implying that all humans are equal and one ought not to divide humans based on religion.[4] This spirit of universal comradeship (brotherhood) and equality became one of the basic principles of Sikhism.

The three pillars of Sikhism that Guru Nanak founded are thus:

Naam Japna: Meditating on the name of God. This is done by reciting the Guru's hymns each day and remembering Him in one's thoughts and deeds.

Kirat Karni: Living an honest and truthful life.

Vand Chakhna: Vand means to share and *Chakhna* means to consume. Sikhs are advised to share their wealth with others. Thus, donating their wealth to the larger community is an essential part of Sikhism.

Guru Gobind Singh and Foundation of the Khalsa

Guru Nanak was succeeded by nine Gurus, the last of whom was Guru Gobind Singh. Born as Gobind Rai to the 9th Sikh Guru, Guru Tegh Bahadur, he would found the Khalsa Panth and give the Sikh faith its current form.

Guru Gobind Singh made the Sikhs a warrior community and stressed on arms training at an early age. He taught the Sikhs to take up arms to fight Mughal injustice. In his own words, as expressed in the Persian poem '*Zaffarnama*',

> When all has been tried, yet
> Justice is not in sight,
> It is then right to pick up the sword,
> It is then right to fight.

The concept of the saint–soldier was born. Sikhs were given the titles of Singh (lion, for men) and Kaur (lioness, for women).

Ever since then, baptised Sikhs were required to keep *kesh* (hair), *kangha* (comb), *kara* (steel bangle), *kachha* (underwear) and *kirpan* (sword) as markers of their initiation into the brotherhood.

Key Tenets of Sikhism

A key tenet of Sikhism is the principle of equality and inclusivity. Sikhs believe that there is one God and all are equal before His eyes. This notion of equality is not only in terms of caste, class, or religion but also extends to notions of gender, beliefs, practices and identities. Another important tenet is *seva* (performing selfless service towards others).

Furthermore, Sikhism encourages the married life of a householder. It encourages people to live and engage in society. The Sikh Gurus did not encourage monasticism, renunciation, celibacy or asceticism.

The five vices that a Sikh is to guard against are *kaam* (lust), *krodh* (anger), *lobh* (greed), *moh* (attachment) and *ahankar* (ego).

Gender Equality in Sikhism

Sikhism regards women to be of an equal status as men in all respects. Women in Sikhism are not barred from any social or religious activity and they can partake in all rituals. The Sikh Gurus led by example by denouncing various practices that debarred women or treated them unequally.

Guru Nanak also condemned the general notion of impurity imputed to women during their menstruation periods.

> From woman, man is born; within woman, man is conceived; to woman he is engaged and married.
>
> Woman becomes his friend; through woman, the future generations come. When his woman dies, he seeks another woman; to woman he is bound.
>
> So why call her bad? From her, kings are born.
>
> From woman, woman is born; without woman, there would be no one at all.

– Raag Aasaa Mehal 1, p. 473, Guru Granth Sahib

These attitudes were among the most progressive towards women for their time and the milieu from which Sikhism emerged. Guru Amar Das worked further towards uplifting women. He condemned the purdah system, which kept women hidden behind a veil in public and away from men, and the sati ritual in which a widow would submit herself into the funeral pyre of her husband; instead, Guru Amar Das advocated widow remarriage and rehabilitation.

Guru Amar Das also appointed 146 people to spread the message of Sikhism; of these, fifty-two were women. Also, the Guru established twenty-two *manjis* (missionaries) to spread Sikhism, of which four were women.

Similar to *manjis*, he established the *piri* system in which women were appointed as leaders to spread the message of the Guru among other women. The *langar* (free community food) is another of his many contributions in which he instated equal treatment for all, irrespective of their caste, class or any other social demarcation. Men and women of all castes sat beside each other as equals during *langar* meals. This ritual symbolically dissolves the boundaries and hierarchies of society and establishes equality.

When Guru Gobind Singh established the Khalsa, women were also baptised by receiving the *amrit*. Since baptised women carried the title of Kaur, it freed them from acquiring the title of their husband. Women were imparted the knowledge of the *shastra* (weapons), which led to many women being trained as warriors in the community.

Halemi Raj: The Sikh View of Governance

Although the Sikh Gurus and Sikh teachings are mostly spiritual, concerning themselves with how to lead an honest life and meet with the True Lord through one's actions, there are also references to what an ideal state rule should be like.

Guru Arjan Dev, the 5th Guru of the Sikhs, wrote a verse which suggests the kind of world held by the Gurus.

> Now, the Merciful Lord has issued His Command.
> Let no one chase after and attack anyone else.
> Let all abide in peace, under this Benevolent Rule. | | *13* | |

This is a world of equality and peace, where no one is chased, attacked or harassed by others for any reason. Guru Arjan Dev talks about the rule of compassion and benevolence. Queer lives can find much comfort and security in this tenet of governance according to Sikhism.

Sikhism on Transgender Issues

According to Sikh teachings, every living being has a soul. Like drops of water separated from the ocean, the *atma* (soul) has been separated from *Paramatma* (God). Like God, the soul is thus formless and genderless.

If one remembers God in one's thoughts and prayers, leads a life according to Sikh beliefs and the path laid down by the Guru, one may attain salvation upon death when the soul can finally merge again with God. Otherwise, the soul passes through 8.4 million different living forms before being reborn as a human in another opportunity to resolve one's karmic burdens.

Since the *atman* is the same that permeates all creation, a transperson can be regarded as metaphysically no different from any other individual. Anybody can attain salvation by following the path laid by the Gurus.

> God created light of which all beings were born.
> And from this light, the universe; so who is good
> and who is bad. The creation is in the Creator.
> And the Creator is in the creation.

This notion of divinity that permeates all creation is reaffirmed in Sikhism repeatedly. For instance, the *bani* points to the perfect diversity present in nature as an intentional manifestation of God.

> The clay is the same, but the designer has fashioned
> it in various ways
> Nothing is wrong with the pot of clay and there is
> nothing wrong with the potter.

The Creator has fashioned living beings differently. This difference could be in the form of race, colour, gender, physical characteristics and sexual orientation. Far from condemning any particular gender variant or sexuality, one could observe that the primary focus of Sikhism is to affirm the equality of all people.

However, unlike Hinduism, which is replete with stories of queer encounters and gender fluidity, the Sikh attitude towards queer individuals can only be surmised through interpretations of teachings and events in the lives of the Gurus. This paucity of references to queer lives is despite the existence of the vibrant *hijra* community in the medieval period under the state patronage of the Mughals.

However, there is one story that refers to a meeting between Guru Nanak and a Sufi saint dressed as a woman. It is narrated in the Janamsakhis, which are a collection of life stories of Guru Nanak written long after his death. They play an important role in Sikh history and theology, as it is through these stories that the life, works and teachings of the Guru are transmitted. The Janamsakhis are not to be regarded as primarily historical documents, however; they include social and cultural myths that emerged over the years and contain descriptions of miracles that occurred during the lifetime of the Guru.

The B40 Janamsakhi contains various stories from Guru Nanak's life, especially one pertaining to a meeting with Sheikh Saraf, a Sufi saint:

During Guru Nanak's visit to Baghdad, he met Sheikh Saraf who was 'wearing the 16 adornments [that a woman traditionally applied to herself in order to attract her lover]. [He was clad in] female garments and arrayed in all manner of jewellery. To his eyes he had applied black eye-shadow (*anjan*) and his hands he had stained red with henna. He sang *ghazals* in the bazaar and drew enormous crowds'. The Guru asked the Sheikh why he was dressed in this manner, to which the Sufi saint replied that since he had not yet found his beloved, he decided to dress as a bride. The Guru observed that the most beloved one is God, for whom external adornments and attire matter not at all: 'If [a man] commits the sins of innumerable existences and then, if the Master so wills, meets one who has attained Truth then he is saved. It is [dependent on] the favour of the Master. Whatever He desires, that He performs'.[5]

And so, the Guru and the Sheikh continued their discourse on the nature of the divine. It is said that they even recited hymns or *ghazals* for each other. This lore, while unlikely to be of a historical nature, hints at the comfort and acceptance

Guru Nanak exhibits during his encounter with a cross-dressing Sufi.

Coming Out in the Sikh Context

Among the five Ks that a Sikh is supposed to value and keep is *kesh* (hair). A Sikh is not encouraged to shave his or her hair, because the human body in its natural form is considered a gift from God. Thus, self-acceptance is central to Sikhism.

Kesh, along with the other four Ks, gives a unique identity to Sikhs. The five Ks and the *dastar* (turban) make a Sikh stand out prominently. Guru Gobind Singh, who commanded that Sikhs keep the five Ks while forming the Khalsa, wanted to create a fearless community that would not be hiding in crowds but would come out in the open and take pride in his or her identity.

The implications for queer individuals struggling with self-acceptance and coming to terms with their identities are clear. Sexual or gender identities are God-ordained matters of human reality. Sikhism teaches one to accept one's self as creations of the perfect God. One could argue, therefore, that accepting one's sexuality is also accepting and respecting His wishes and forms.

Moreover, Sikhism has never viewed sexuality as a hindrance in the path to being one with God. Sikhism has always valued the householder's life over the hermit's. Marriage and family are seen as foundations of society. It is this acceptance of sexuality by the Gurus that led them to promote *grishti jeevan* (married life), unlike some other religions that view sexuality and the householder's life as distractions in the pursuit of salvation or enlightenment.

Marriages in Sikhism

Marriage in the Sikh faith does not specify the gender of the individuals getting married. Instead, marriage is a unification of the human soul, *atman*, with the Creator, *Para-atman*. The marriage ceremony is called Anand Karaj, meaning blissful union, and involves the couple walking around the Guru Granth Sahib four times, with the four verses of the hymns (*lavan*) being sung in the background.

The four stanzas of *lavan* were written by Guru Ram Das, the fourth Sikh Guru. They refer to the human soul as the bride and God as the groom. The hymns outline the progressive stages of the awakening soul-bride as she advances spiritually to ultimately blend with the divine groom in the dawning realisation of her divine destiny.[6]

The four hymns are:

> In the first round of the marriage ceremony, the Lord gives you His instructions for married life. Instead of performing rituals by routine, embrace the righteous life of Dharma, and do nothing that separates you from God. Meditate on God's Name.

I Am Divine. So Are You.

Embrace and practise Simran – the continuous remembrance of your True Identity. Worship and adore the Guru, the Perfect True Guru, and all the errors of your past shall be washed away. By your great destiny, you shall know that bliss which passes all understanding, and the Lord – Har, Har, will become sweet to your mind. Servant Nanak proclaims that in this first round, the marriage ceremony has begun.

In the second round of the marriage ceremony, the Lord guides you to meet the True Guru – the One Teacher. Filled with the awe of the Infinite, your ego dissolves away. In awe of the One who is forever pure, sing His Wonderful Praises and see God in all. The Lord – the Supreme Soul – is the Master of the Universe. He fills everything, everywhere. He fills all spaces. Deep within you, and outside you as well, see only One God. God's humble servants meet together and sing the songs of joy and ecstasy. Servant Nanak proclaims that in this second round, the music of the spheres resounds.

In the third round of the marriage ceremony your heart is filled with Divine Love. By my great destiny I have met the humble Saints who love the Lord and I have found God. I have found the pure

Lord and I sing His Wonderful Praises. I sing the Guru's Bani. By great good destiny I have found the humble Saints and I speak in the silent language of the Infinite. The Lord's Name – Har, Har, Har – vibrates and resounds within my heart. Meditating on God, I have realised the great destiny written on my forehead. Servant Nanak proclaims that in this third round, the heart is full of Divine Love of the One God.

In the fourth round of the marriage ceremony I have found God and my mind is filled with peace. Living as a Gurmukh, I have met Him with simple ease. My mind and body are full of sweet delight. I am pleasing to God – and night and day I lovingly focus my awareness on Him. I have merged with the One in everyone and all my desires are fulfilled. The Lord's Name resounds and reverberates within me and all around me. The One God, my Lord and Master, merges with His Divine Bride and her heart blossoms with His Holy Name. Servant Nanak proclaims that in this fourth round, we have become One with the Eternal Lord.

Observe that the *lavans* use the feminine pronoun to refer to the human soul (of both the bride and the groom). This makes the Sikh marriage ritual gender-neutral and equal in treatment of both sexes.

I Am Divine. So Are You.

Modern Sikh Responses to the Queer

The Sikh leadership in India has unfortunately been uncomfortable with the queer. When the Supreme Court of India upheld Section 377 of the Indian Penal Code criminalizing homosexuality, leaders from various religions welcomed the judgement and issued a joint statement warning the Government of India against decriminalising homosexuality in India. One of the signatories to this statement was Gyani Ranjit Singh, the chief priest of Bangla Sahib Gurudwara in New Delhi.[7]

This was not an exception, however. The Akal Takht, the spiritual and temporal authority of Sikhism, has consistently opposed same-sex marriage. In 2005, when the Canadian Parliament introduced a bill to legalise same-sex marriages in the country, the head priest of Akal Takht, Jathedar Joginder Singh Vedanti, asked Sikhs in Canada to oppose the law.[8]

In 2016, when Ontario Premier Kathleeen Wynne, who is openly lesbian and a strong advocate of same-sex marriages, visited the Golden Temple in Amritsar – the holiest shrine in Sikhism – the governing body of the temples decided not to honour her with a *siropa* (robe) because of her position on same-sex marriage.[9]

However, now with a sizeable population of Sikhs in the West, there have been support groups for LGBT Sikhs to help them come out and at the same time reconcile their faith with their leadership's positions. Sarbat (www.sarbat.net) is a UK-based

LGBT support group for Sikhs. They have online resources and information for LGBT Sikhs across the globe. They also hold local meets and events for LGBT Sikhs in the UK.

LGBT Sikhs under the banner of Sarbat also took part in the gay pride parade in UK in 2015. Similarly, there have been other individual efforts by gay Sikhs to address the issue of homosexuality and Sikhism and help in the acceptance of LGBT Sikhs by their families. Manjinder Singh, a UK-based Sikh who comes out with videos on spirituality and lifestyle, had his mother speak out in Punjabi in one of the videos. She urged other parents to accept their gay children.

Sher Vancouver is another Canada-based group for LGBTQ South Asians. Although it started out as an LGBT support group for Sikhs in Canada, it soon transformed into a support group for South Asian queers.[10]

Sikh Religion and Punjabi Culture

In a discussion about the religion of Sikhism and the discomfort with the queer among its current leadership, it is important to separate the folk culture of the people from the tenets of Sikhism.

Sikhism flourished in the northern Indian state of Punjab and has a great influence on many of the cultural aspects of the people who live there. Like any culture, the Punjabi culture also not only embodies the dominant religious practices of the faith but also includes aspects that are influenced by time, social norms and more. For instance, despite the complete rejection of the caste system and inequality between the sexes in Sikhism, these ills have crept back into the practices of its people in the Punjab region. The state of Punjab has one of the most disparate gender ratios in India due to sex selection and preference for a male child. Further, in a practice that appears to contradict the central thrust of Sikhism, women are prohibited from singing the holy hymns inside the Golden Temple of Amritsar. Like much of northern India, Punjab remains a deeply patriarchal society, which often manifests itself in hyper-masculine behaviour.

The Sikh leadership of the Akal Takht and members of the governing body of the gurudwaras are mostly products of this cultural milieu. This colours their interpretations of Sikh teachings to a significant extent, especially in the face of the fact that none of the holy scriptures of Sikhism directly tackle the issues of queer realities.

Conclusion: A Probable Way Forward

Thus, it remains to be seen how this young faith evolves over the years. The founding principles of equality, inclusivity, peace and self-acceptance are critical to its identity among the Karmic faiths.

The 9th Guru of the Sikhs, Guru Teg Bahadur, sacrificed his life for the rights of a persecuted minority (the Hindus) during the Mughal reign. There is little reason why the Sikh faith could not stand up once again in support of any other persecuted minority today. This is the basic calling of Sikh men and women as brave lions and lionesses who are always willing and ready to combat injustice. One can argue that this willingness to combat oppression can be extended in a gesture of not only compassion but also consistent application of its key tenets to affirm the dignity of queer lives in Sikhism.

Some online resources for LGBT Sikhs:
Sarbat: www.sarbat.net
Gay Sikh: www.gaysikh.com
Sher Vancouver: www.shervancouver.com
Gaylaxy: www.gaylaxymag.com/tag/sikhism/

5

Hinduism: The Wise See Diversity

By Jerry Johnson
With inputs from Devdutt Pattanaik and
Dr Meera Baindur

- Key Principles of Hinduism
- Diversity and the Queer in Hinduism
- Discomfort with the Queer in Hinduism
- Queer as Part of Hindu Faith/Culture/Scriptures
- A New Informed Engagement
- Coming Out
- Dealing with Rejection
- Conclusion

Vishwarupa: God revealing Himself as the container as well as content of all that exists. Based on the Bhagavad Gita, this image expresses the essential Hindu theme of diversity and universal divinity. *(Source: Wikimedia Commons)*

Hinduism refers to the various streams of beliefs that originated and developed over 4,000 years in the South Asian subcontinental region. The term originally implied a geographic, ethnic or cultural identifier for people living around and beyond the Indus river. Over time, it also came to refer to the religious belief systems of the native people. These religious belief systems include: Shaivism, Vaishnavism, Shaktism, Shrauta, Smarta, Vedanta, Tantra, Bhakti and various reform and contemporary movements of the late 19th and early 20th century, such as Arya Samaj, Ramakrishna Mission, Chinmaya Mission and ISKCON (International Society of Krishna Consciousness).

However, there is no single, comprehensive doctrine shared by all Hindus. Hinduism is a network of overlapping beliefs and rituals that share some resemblance with each other and serve as markers of the religion. Importantly, there is no single, consistent system of theological belief in any one God. Hinduism has no uniquely authoritative scripture to the exclusion of other sacred scriptures. It does not have an authoritative college of clergy to expound upon its basic principles for all Hindus, and it does not have a singular concept of divinity that is accepted by all.

In a compelling sense, Hinduism can be understood less as a religious doctrine and more like a philosophical framework about life, death, the world and human relationships.

Scholars of Indian philosophy typically understand the term 'Hinduism' as standing for the collection of philosophical or metaphysical views that share a textual connection to certain core Hindu scriptures. These include the Vedas, the Bhagavad Gita and the epics Ramayana and Mahabharata, and they do not identify Hinduism with a particular comprehensive dogma.

Hinduism, thus understood, includes doctrines and beliefs emerging from numerous sources – from reflections of sages and dialogues of seers to poetic meditations and sacred chants. The body of Hindu philosophy even incorporates the schools of atheistic thought (*nastika*), such as of Carvaka and Samkhya, which upheld an epistemology of direct perception, empiricism, inference, reliabilism and scepticism.

Evolving over millennia as a dynamic response to the events occurring in societies at the time, Hinduism developed as a fusion, expansion or rejection of older beliefs. Moreover, given the large number of scriptures and sources of tradition that constitute Hinduism, one finds significant variations and differing implications of the beliefs in practice across time, region and cultures in the subcontinent.

Ultimately, what matters to the Hindu is the spiritual experience or the ritual. Indeed, it is believed that the world of matter and the world of the soul are mediated through the world of ritual practices. This is why Hinduism has a rich tradition spanning millennia of ritual chants or the discourse of the gurus or the poetry of the Vedic sages being transmitted not in written form but in oral hymns and recitations repeated in sacred gatherings.

Over the years, Hinduism partook in continuous reciprocal engagement with concurrent streams of thought flowing in the Indian subcontinent, such as Buddhism, Jainism and, later, Islam and Christianity.

Key Principles of Hinduism

Hinduism must be understood as a continuously adapting system of beliefs with a few central principles in constant interplay with one another.

Rebirth

The Hindu metaphysic holds that the universe is non-dual, eternal and infinite. The embodied '*atman*' (loosely translated as 'soul') merely changes forms through infinite time. At every birth, the *atman* is embodied in a new form: human, non-human or animal. Hence, human beings, who are materially embodied forms of the *atman*, undergo cycles of rebirth over time.

This movement of the soul through endless forms and an eternity of lifetimes is called *samsara*, which means wandering from one life on to the next, and suggesting an emotional experience of uncertainty and helplessness.

The phenomenon of rebirth is articulated in great detail in one of the earliest central scriptures of Hindu philosophy, the *Brihadaranyaka Upanishad* – a treatise on the soul – estimated to have been composed around 700 BCE:

After death, the soul goes to the next world, bearing in mind the subtle impressions of its deeds, and after reaping their harvest returns again to this world of action. Thus, he is subjected to continuous rebirth.

– Yajur Veda, Brihadaranyaka Upanishad 4.4.6

Karma

The force that propels the *atman* from one form to another over an eternity of lifetimes is karma. In the simplest sense, karma can be understood as the principle of action and consequence; or, in terms familiar to Western philosophy, it can be understood as the law of causality that governs how an entity acts. Since the Hindu metaphysical universe is infinite, the canvas of causality that animates the *atman* through it is therefore also infinite. Hinduism thus rejects the notion of the First Cause.

According to Hinduism, the actions of the embodied *atman* set in motion in the countless previous lives form the tendencies and conditions of the embodied *atman* in its next life. Each action's consequences must run their full course even across multiple lifetimes in order for the karmic burden to be resolved. It is only when all karmic burden is resolved or when the true nature of the *atman* is understood and the 'I' that acts is dissolved that the cycle of rebirth comes to an end and the *atman* is liberated from further embodiment. This attainment of liberation is called *moksha*.

Dharma

The other principle central to Hinduism is the concept of dharma, and it is closely linked with the concept of karma.

Dharma can be understood as contextually appropriate behaviour or righteous conduct, but what that would mean varies greatly according to person, context and karmic accumulation. In a metaphysic governed by karmic rebirth, the interplay between the principles of karma and dharma is complex. At the risk of simplicity, however, if karma is understood as the propelling force of causality across lifetimes, dharma can be understood as the law of identity (or the essential nature of an entity or the embodied *atman*) in the present lifetime.

Thus understood, as an entity *is* so will it *behave*. As is the *form* of the *atman*, so are its *actions*.

In the context of plants and animals, this becomes a fairly deterministic description of reality: the nature of a plant/animal determines the actions it can take. This is seen as the 'dharma' of the plant/animal.

Dharma is to humans what natural behaviour is to a plant or animal. However, since human beings are entities with imagination, agency and intentionality, an individual's dharma (appropriate behaviour) becomes a matter of ethical choice, context, wisdom and purpose. One's dharma or dharmic action is therefore often mired in complexities and dilemmas (*dharma-sankat*). Indeed, one of the central wisdoms of Hindu thought is that being truly human is to have to confront and grapple with dharmic complexities and be able to glean ethical wisdom from these experiences. In contrast, the word for the Supreme Divinity in Sanskrit is '*bhagavan*', which can be understood as referring to a being who has infinite wisdom over all complexities.

The idea that humans, in contrast to *bhagavan*, are inherently limited in perspective becomes of critical importance in understanding some of the central messages of Hinduism. While there is little to no scope for a plant or animal to resolve accumulated karmic burden through the cessation of action, or for it to discover the true nature of the *atman*, it is wholly incumbent upon humans to discover their dharma and act according to it in order to attain liberation.

Traditionally, this involved doing one's duty as child, spouse, parent, or a member of the caste (*jati*). It involved undergoing the rites of passage, which included marrying, raising a family, carrying forward the family vocation, caring for the elders, and repaying one's karmic debts (*rinn*) owed to one's own caste community, village, sages, gods and ancestors.

In recent times, dharma has also come to mean duty or the righteous path in some interpretations; and the Indian Constitution uses the word 'dharma' to refer to one's religion.

Yagna

Another feature unique to Hinduism is not so much a principle as it is a ritual. Over 3,000 years ago, mystic sages in the Indian subcontinent described a fire ritual known as the *yagna*. Transmitted orally and over time, constituting what we now know as the Vedas, these early hymns describe a ritual in which an offering is made into the fire in order to summon a deity and seek the fulfilment of desires in return.

Karma and dharma gain significant meaning in the ritual action of *yagna*. Karma is referred to as both action and reaction in a *yagna* ritual, while dharma is referred to as one of the duties of a Hindu man to perform this ritual.

Western scholars have typically translated this Vedic fire ritual as a sacrificial offering – wherein a sacrifice is made to the fire to please the gods – because of its familiar resemblance to Biblical stories of sacrificial offerings to the Abrahamic God.

However, mythologist Dr Devdutt Pattanaik has argued that this ritual can be properly understood as an 'exchange' or 'trade' between entities. Hence, the ubiquitous concept of debt (*rinn*) that binds humans to society and the material world, at large. Many of the hymns, for instance, ask for special favours from deities in exchange for offerings, such as requests for worldly rewards of economic prosperity (*artha*) or sensual pleasures (*kama*) that come from pleasing the gods.

As Vedic Hinduism transformed into Puranic Hinduism and as Vedic fire altars gave way to Hindu temples, the ritual of *yagna* transformed into the ritual of *puja*, where flowers, incense and light are offered to the enshrined deity in exchange for grace.

Thus, the principle of exchange continues in a new form.

Funeral Rites

Of particular significance to our purpose here are the rites of passage associated with the end of life, funeral and death (*antyeshti* or *shraadh*). Since according to Hinduism infinite rebirth is a metaphysical reality, each person bears a karmic debt (*rinn*) to his or her deceased ancestors to bear offspring who would serve as vehicles for their subsequent rebirths.

Therefore, a Hindu man is expected to perform the ritual called *shraadh* for his deceased ancestors, during which he offers rice cakes to crows (symbolising his ancestors) and promises to produce children to facilitate their rebirth. Failing to facilitate rebirth is seen as shunning one's responsibility (or shirking off one's karmic debt) to the souls of one's ancestors due to whom one is currently alive. Worse still, it is depriving one's own ancestors of yet another opportunity to resolve their own karmic burdens in a new lifetime. Thus, procreation is understood as a crucial dharmic function of a Hindu man.

This ritual of 'metaphysical trade' (or *yagna*) to pay off karmic debt continues to inform social attitudes towards queer sexuality – especially that of Hindu gay men – as a core obligation (dharma) of their householder life. Hence, in many Hindu families, heterosexual marriages and producing children are not seen as problematic repressions of one's gay identity but as a fulfilment of one's dharmic duty as the male member of the household. The patriarchal privileges of this asymmetric arrangement accorded only to men, unfortunately, continue to be taken for granted uncritically in modern India.

Diversity and the Queer in Hinduism

In Karmic faiths, actions from a previous life or lives often necessitate a certain physical form in the next birth. Because the soul is immortal and the body it chooses to inhabit is mortal and temporary, Karmic faiths accommodate a huge variety of individual bodies as a natural consequence of the outcomes of actions performed in previous lifetimes (karma). As a result, these bodies that one's soul occupies may be of any form – human, non-human or not entirely human.

This physical body is already endowed with a pre-provided set of psycho-sexual attributes that will manifest in its lifetime. Gender identity is one such pre-determined attribute. The immortal soul, however, has no gender and no orientation. The psycho-sexual body is the seat of emotions, desires, propensities, orientations and also of moral agency. Drawing from this we can have a psycho-sexual woman stuck in a physically male body or vice versa and we can have a variety of orientations that the psycho-sexual body inherits as a consequence of its own karmic past:

> In every body resides the divine who witnesses, guides, supports and enjoys all that the body experiences.
>
> — Bhagavad Gita, Chapter 13, Verse 22

Even the gods and goddesses in Hindu mythic stories exhibit gender fluidity and queer orientations. In the post-Vedic period over 2,000 years ago, a new kind of Hinduism emerged, which carried tales of gods, kings and sages who were able to reduce karmic burden without renouncing society or abandoning the *yagna* rituals. These stories propounded the virtues of following one's dharma. Stories of Shiva and his children, Vishnu and his *avatars* such as Ram and Krishna, and Shakti and her myriad manifestations started being chronicled in Sanskrit texts known as Puranas, from which we get the term 'Puranic Hinduism'.

During this period, many stories emerged wherein gods transition into goddesses and vice versa. There are gods who are third-gendered and some that manifest all three genders. Some deities only cross-dress, without gender transition.

Then there are male gods who exhibit female attributes and female gods with male attributes. In the Bhagavad Gita, Lord Krishna refers to matter (*prakriti*) and the mind (*purusha*) as his two wombs (*yoni*).[1] In some stories, Krishna is described as tying his hair in a plait, decorating his palms with red dye, wearing a nose-ring, and bending his body gracefully.[2] It is in this form that Krishna is called the best of men (*purushottama*) and the complete man (*purna-purusha*). Apparently, for the ancients, masculinity did not diminish when the feminine was amplified.

One of the most celebrated forms of Lord Vishnu even today is the one in which he takes the form of the beautiful damsel Mohini to seduce, dupe and then kill the *asuras*. This

I Am Divine. So Are You.

form is regularly taken out in processions during Vishnu temple ceremonies such as Brahmotsavam.

Similarly, a female form of Lord Shiva in which he assumes the body of a milkmaid so that he can dance around Krishna in the paradise of cows (*gau-loka*) is also worshipped today as the milkmaid God or Gopeshwar Mahadev in Mathura.

For their part, goddesses are often shown only in the company of other goddesses, riding lions and going into battle with a trident in hand – characteristics that some would regard as masculine. Female deities in Hinduism are autonomous and look upon their male counterparts as objects of pleasure or the means to produce progeny.[3] The Goddess is mother and daughter at the same time. In Goddess temples, she is either enshrined alone or with a female companion, or with two male consorts. In God temples, she is enshrined with the male deity as a consort, but often in a separate independent shrine, as we find in temples of Krishna-Vishnu in Puri, Tirumalai, Pandharpur and Dwaraka.

The epic story of the Mahabharata includes many queer characters such as Brihanalla, a man who loses his manhood for a year. Shikhandi is a woman who secures male genitalia later in life. Bhagashavana lives part of his or her life as a man, husband and father and the rest as woman, wife and mother. Yuvanashva, who drinks a magic potion, becomes pregnant and delivers a son from his thigh. Ila's masculinity waxes and wanes with the moon, and Aravan's wife is Mohini, the female form of Krishna-Vishnu.

Aravan, a deity worshipped in northern Tamil Nadu and Pondicherry. During the epic Kurukshetra war, this son of Arjuna had to be sacrificed to the Goddess. He wanted to marry on the eve of his sacrifice, but no woman agreed to be married to a man who would die the next day and make them widows. So Krishna, a God, took the form of a woman and chose to become his wife and, eventually, his wailing widow. Aravan came to be worshipped as the incarnate form of Shiva, and became the husband of all transgendered people in this region, who call themselves Aravani, the wife of Aravan. *(Source: Wikimedia Commons)*

The Puranas have stories of intimate relationships between members of the same sex, such as the story of Somavat and Sumedha, who marry after one of them turns into a woman.

Regional folk retellings of the Ramayana often put a queer spin on some of the central characters of the epic. For example, Aruna, the God of dawn, is described as being of indeterminate gender, as he was born prematurely. He chooses to become a woman and is impregnated by two male Gods, Indra and Surya.[4]

I Am Divine. So Are You.

Similarly, the *hijras*, in a version of the Ramayana, talk about the episode when Ram returns to his kingdom after his fourteen-year exile and finds them waiting for him outside the gates of Ayodhya. Ram asks them for an explanation and the *hijras* reply: 'When you were leaving, the people of Ayodhya wanted to follow you to the forest. But you ordered the men and women to return to the city. We are neither men nor women and so we did not know what your instructions were for us. So we waited here for you to return and tell us.' Moved by this display of unconditional devotion, Ram promised the *hijras* that they would be respected in Kali-yuga (the current times) and he welcomed them into his city.

In the Tulsi Ramcharitmanas (7.87ka), the most popular Ramayana in north India, Ram tells the crow Bhusandi, *'Purush napunsaka nari va jiva charachara koi, sarva bhaav bhaja kapat taji mohi param priya soi.'* ('Men, queers, women, animals or plants who approach me after abandoning malice are beloved to me.') Here, Lord Ram is making himself accessible to all living beings, even the queer (*napunsaka*).

All of these descriptions of inherent fluidity and diversity in physical bodies demonstrate the remarkable comfort with the queer found among the Hindu gods and narrated in their mythologies. One must be careful, however, to not read these stories as mere superficial endorsements of queer realities. Instead, they must be seen as metaphorical vehicles employed by the ancients to communicate complex ideas of metaphysics, sexuality, diversity and human nature in narrative and symbolic form.

Goddess Bahuchara, from the state of Gujarat, is shown here riding a rooster. During the *hijra* castration ritual, the name of this Goddess is invoked. In temple lore, she was the wife of a man who wanted to be a woman. She was furious when she found this out and cursed her husband and demanded that men like him should turn into *hijras* and worship her. The *hijra* priestesses who worship this Goddess are sometimes referred to as Mangal-mukhi, or auspicious ones. Some of them embrace celibacy. *(Source: Wikimedia Commons)*

For instance, the image of Ardha-Nareshwara, the half-woman God, can indicate a queer form of a person like a *hijra*, or it can perhaps indicate the union of the mind (God) and matter (Goddess) creating a complete whole, therefore suggesting the holistic unity and internality of the universe, or it can indicate the incompleteness of the masculine principle without the equally animating force of the feminine principle.

Moreover, the vocabulary used to describe these

I Am Divine. So Are You.

metaphysical themes – in modern translation – may appear to fall short of what contemporary society would consider polite or politically correct. A direct translation of these words suggests that the queer are less than men, not quite women, and therefore incomplete. For instance, *'Na-punsaka'* means 'non-man' while *'kin-nara'* means 'what-man' and finds its mention in the scriptures referring to special beings that stand alongside the gods, demons and sages. The term *hijra* serves as a catch-all phrase for the traditional transgender communities of India. The term has its origins in the Islamic culture and Mughal courts, even though many *hijras* also hold faith in various Hindu deities. For example, in Tamil Nadu there are transgenders who are known as the Aravanis because of their fealty to the deity Aravan; in Karnataka, there are the Jogatas who are linked to the deity Renuka-Yellamma; in Gujarat and north India, one finds the Mangal-mukhi community that is closely associated with the Goddess Bahuchara. In recent times, the word *kinnara* is being increasingly used to refer to transgenders who are seeking mainstream Hindu assimilation.

In 2016, a *kinnara akhara* (loosely translated to a particular place of practice, worship or rituals founded by transgendered priests) was established during the Ujjain Kumbha Mela, headed by the well-known transgender rights activist Lakshmi Narayan Tripathi. At the founding ceremony, Tripathi was anointed as the Acharya Mahamandaleshwar (pontiff) of the *akhara*, with the blessings of various Hindu leaders including the Shankaracharyas, revealing a gradual mainstreaming of these otherwise marginalised communities.[5] This venture is also helping bridge the gap between the transgenders and the wider LGBQ community, the former being seen as the more traditional expression of the queer in Indian culture and the latter as its modern manifestation.

All of these various terms to describe the queer can lead us to a charitable interpretation that the ancients grappled with having to articulate queer truths with a heteronormative vocabulary and template that was most familiar to them.

Nevertheless, it is noteworthy to contrast this sheer abundance of stories of queer diversity with the near absence of tales of either cross-dressing, gender transitioning or same-sex love in the Bible or the Quran. Further, none of the Puranic scriptures have tales resembling that of Sodom and Gomorrah, which have been popularly interpreted as divine punishment for queer behaviour.

Indeed, the very idea of 'homosexuality as sin' is absent from the Hindu corpus, as it does not conceptually fit within a metaphysic of karma and infinite rebirth.

Discomfort with the Queer in Hinduism

An important factor that influences the queer perspective in Hinduism is the persistent and problematic preference for male progeny. This tendency may have originated in the ancient funeral ritual of *shraadh* described earlier, wherein the male progeny would light the funeral pyre of his deceased ancestor as a means to liberate its soul from the body and proceed on to its next birth.

This ritual persists in contemporary society, and the cultural associations around male privilege continue. Indeed, the word for son in Sanskrit is *'putra'*, which also refers to the person who 'saves one from the hell reserved for where the childless go' (Verse 38, Chapter 74, Adi Parva of the Mahabharata).

Therefore, the dharmic function of married couples is to produce progeny – preferably male – toth facilitate subsequent rebirth, without which ultimate liberation is unattainable. The inability to fulfil this critical dharmic function – which is tied to the karmic purpose of death and rebirth – is therefore used as a justification to perceive homosexual and queer manifestations as inferior, wasteful or undesirable. Indeed, transgendered persons and infertile men are derogatively called *'kliba'* in some texts as a way to identify them for being 'not man enough'.

The injunction to produce offspring is so emphatic in Hinduism that if one is unable to produce one's own children, the wife is even permitted to cohabit with other men until she bears a child for her husband. For instance, in the scriptures Pandu calls upon the gods to inseminate his wife and produce offsprings, who go on to then become the central protagonists of the great epic Mahabharata.

In the *Manusmriti*, which literally means 'the reflections of Manu' and is the oldest articulation of the codes of conduct to be followed by a Hindu, homosexuality is frowned upon mildly due to its 'wasteful' character. It must be kept in mind that *Manusmriti* is one of the many albeit most popular dharmashastras, which became significant after the British chose it to base their design of the legal system of India, especially in matters of Hindu personal law. Its value in governing the ethics of Hindu society, prior to British intervention, has been challenged by scholars.[6] Hinduism has no paradigm of 'sin' under which it locates homosexuality. The punishment for sex between men has less to do with the act and more to do with the compromises on their duties as householders. Sometimes it is also proscribed because of the castes of the men involved. In Manu's view, homosexual behaviour is a wasteful act of lust or desire that increases one's karmic burden because it is not a productive act of procreation that fulfils one's dharmic functions. It equates homosexual sex to a man having sex with a menstruating woman, or having sex during the day.[7]

As a result, we find that male homoerotic desire was historically not punished with dire consequences. Homosexual behaviour among ordinary males of the upper castes was classified as a minor offence for which a ritual bathing was prescribed.

In the case of female homosexuality, the act was punishable only if the girls involved were virgins. The punishment in such a case was severe for the older woman – '[who] shall instantly have her head shaved or two fingers cut off, and be made to ride on a donkey'.[8] Similarly, the punishment for a forced act of heterosexual sex with a virgin was also severe. In contrast, female homosexuality among two virgin girls was tolerated with mild admonishment. These prescriptions reveal

I Am Divine. So Are You.

an obsession with virginity and the loss of it that rendered a young girl unworthy of marriage rather than any aversion to homosexuality as such.

In contrast, the monastic orders of Hinduism renounced not only the material world but also sexual desire. Semen retention, according to tantric sects and other traditional alchemical texts, was believed to proffer magical powers and hence had to be retained under self-control. As legend goes, Adi Shankaracharya, the fountainhead of Hindu monastic orders, was once asked by the wife of a Sanskrit scholar how he could consider himself knowledgeable about the world if he had never had the knowledge of sexual pleasure. In response, Shankaracharya used his yogic powers to reanimate the corpse of a king and have sexual pleasure with the king's wives. In this way, the story goes, he gained the knowledge of a sexual experience but maintained the purity of his body.[9]

This relegation of physical pleasures as wasteful may explain why queer people continue to be seen as inferior adulterations of the masculine and feminine principles, to be kept out of monasteries, where they may be seen as temptations, and from married society, where they may be seen as irrelevant.

Now, in addition to the internal logic of these doctrines, the beliefs of migrants from Afghanistan, Persia and Europe had an enduring influence on these faiths and shaped their framing of queer expressions. The prevailing attitude of Islam had time was to publicly disavow homosexual behaviour. Muslim migrants also brought with them the practice of castrating some of their male servants. The castrated slaves were considered to be the most reliable and trustworthy of servants since they did not marry and raise families of their own and posed no threat to the Sultan's harems or wives. This tradition of castrated slaves in the courts of Islamic rulers is the precursor to the modern-day *hijra* culture and the traditional transgender community system in India – a self-formed community of transgendered individuals existing at the margins of society and wherein the cultural legacy of Islam continues to be evident.

Queer as Part of Hindu Faith/Culture/Scriptures

As noted in previous sections, ancient scriptures from the subcontinent have variously discussed sexuality in general and queer expressions in particular. Indeed, these may perhaps be the earliest attempts to describe human sexuality and identity in naturalistic terms that approach a scientific articulation. Some of the more prominent examples of these include the *Sushruta Samhita* from 600 BC, the *Caraka Samhita* from around 200 BC, the reflections of Narada in the 1st century BC and the most famous *Kama Sutra* from the 6th century AD.

The *Sushruta Samhita* lists several types of men who are impotent with women and referred to as *kliba* and goes into great detail regarding their distinguishing features in sexual attraction. It asserts that the homosexual *asekya* is conceived as a result of the father's semen being scarce and he therefore enjoys swallowing the semen of other men. The transgender *shandha* is conceived when the mother plays the dominant role during intercourse (*purushayita* or 'woman on top').[10]

The text goes on to assert that all three natures – male, female and the third sex – are determined at the time of conception.

The *Caraka Samhita*, which is an ancient Vedic medical text, lists eight types of men who are unable to copulate with women.

1. *Dviretas* – born with both male and female 'seed'

2. *Pavanendriya* – unable to discharge semen

3. *Samskaravahi* – aroused according to previous life impressions

4. *Narashandha* – manhood is completely destroyed

5. *Narishandha* – womanhood is completely destroyed

6. *Vakri* – penis is severely curved or deformed

7. *Irshyabhirati* – aroused only by seeing others in the act of sexual union

8. *Vatika* – born without testicles.

The text asserts that these variations are produced by unchangeable factors such as previous life impressions, parental conditions and certain conditions within the womb. It is thus one of the earliest claims in the world of a biological basis for homosexuality.

In the *Narada-Smriti*, the sage Narada identifies fourteen different types of men who are impotent with women. These include the *mukhebhaga* (men who have oral sex with other men), the *sevyaka* (men who are sexually enjoyed by other men) and the *irshyaka* (the voyeur who watches other men engaging in sex). All three types are declared unchangeable and are forbidden from marrying women.

The *Kama Sutra* composed by Vatsyayana is the most famous ancient text that deals most freely with desire. It accepts sexual activity as the central theme of our lives as human beings and gives desire, particularly the desire of the body and senses, its rightful place as a human activity. The text can be said to be more worldly-wise and inclusive.

For instance, in its discussion of oral sex between men, the *Kama Sutra* uses the term *tritiya-prakriti* (third sex or third nature) to define men with homosexual desire and describes their practices in great detail. It divides such men into two types: those with a feminine appearance and demeanour, and those having a manly appearance with beards, moustaches, muscular builds and more. The *Kama Sutra* also mentions homosexual marriages based on 'great attachment and complete faith in one another'.

Women who are impotent with men are mentioned less frequently in Vedic literature. Nevertheless, at least ten different types of third-gender women can be found in various Sanskrit texts. The *Kama Sutra* does mention the *svairini* (an independent woman), who engages in aggressive love-making with other women. Lesbians and women who are masculine are mentioned for their skills as businesswomen (*vaisyas*), armed military guards, domestic servants and courtesans. Bisexual women, *kamini*, are described as those who enjoy love-making with both men and women. Some other descriptions of women found in Sanskrit texts are *stripumsa*, a woman with masculine behaviour and form, and *shandhi*, a woman who is averse to men and has no breasts.[11]

Interestingly, the *Kama Sutra* emerges at a time when monastic Buddhism wanes across the subcontinent and Vedic Hinduism – with its penchant for festivities, rituals, social engagement and exchange – enjoys a resurgence through the construction of Hindu temples. Many of these temples openly celebrate erotic imagery and sexuality in their architecture, including many that depicted homosexuality. The temples of Khajuraho and Chapri are striking examples of this. One of the sculpures at the Visvanatha temple of Khajuraho depicts a monk gently caressing a layman.

In fact, many of these temples and their priests nurtured an ecosystem of bustling trade, theatre, art and sexual exploration in the surrounding communities. These temples were seen as celebration of life, light and *kama*, from which comes all of creation. A temple devoid of the depictions of sexuality and sensuality was considered inferior and tantamount to the 'lair of death' and darkness.[12] These facts indicate at the very least that sexual diversity and gender-fluidity were recognised as an evident feature of the world and its discussion or depictions were not considered taboo.

Under Tantric Hinduism, according to which semen retention was thought to engender supernatural or magical powers, third-gendered individuals were considered to hold special powers to bless or curse others. Their powers were proactively sought by members of the heterosexual community for special occasions like blessing a newborn or sanctifying the marriage of newlyweds.

In some instances, the ancient books seem outright progressive in their protection of homosexuals and the third-gendered from abuse by the general public. The *Arthashastra* instructs parents to provide the basic necessities of food and clothing to their third-gender offspring and not neglect their needs. It goes on to state that in cases where there are no relatives, the king must assume responsibility for such individuals. The *Arthashastra* also declares it an offence to vilify or publicly mock any person of the third gender and lists various punitive fines for such offences.

Even among the gods, there are a few examples of explicit homoerotic intimacy. Among the most popular stories is that of the water gods Varuna and Mitra. In the ancient scripture of the *Shatapatha Brahmana*, Mitra is described as 'implanting his seed' into Varuna on every new moon night in order to secure the moon's waning. The text reads like a gentle ode to the moon recited in terms of a homosexual union.

Another account from the *Skanda Purana* involves the fire-god Agni, who on one occasion swallows the semen of Shiva while disguised as an ascetic. In a narrative found in both the *Padma Purana* and Krittivasa Ramayana, the god Shiva commands two queens to make love with each other, after which they conceive a child.[13]

Notably, the deep and intimate same-sex attachments between the gods and their devotees are often described in great detail. Some Hindu scriptures describe these attachments in terms stronger than that held for family members, spouses or anyone else in the entire world.

So, while we can admit that in pre-colonial subcontinental thought, homosexuals did not share an equal status with heterosexual counterparts, the evidence suggests that homosexuals and gender-queers were widely recognised. Their existence was acknowledged and studied. They were at the least tolerated if not accepted as an expression of natural diversity in the world.

This view is further validated when placed within the larger metaphysical narrative of Hinduism articulated in the *Rig Veda: vikriti evam prakriti*, which means that what seems unnatural is also natural, or diversity is nature.

A New Informed Engagement

A central tenet of Karmic faiths is the search for wisdom, hence the multiple lifetimes through which to progressively grow in wisdom. The words for 'what', 'where', 'how', 'why' in Hindi all share the same Sanskrit root 'ka'. Ancient texts also reveal that 'ka' is among the earliest names given to God in Hinduism. Finally, we also see that 'ka' is the same root of the word 'karma' – the force that drives the infinite cycle of birth and rebirth.[14]

Earlier in this chapter, we discussed how the central ritual of a traditional Hindu man was to perform the funeral *yagna* called *shraadh*, where he would feed rice cakes to crows, symbolising his ancestors. Typically, in Hindi, the sound a crow makes is described as 'ka' – which in a Vedic chant would closely resemble the name of God and hint at the principle of karma.

If we connect the dots, we realise the important connections being made between critical thinking, seeking understanding, growing in wisdom and the fundamental metaphysical force that propels one from birth to birth. Perhaps our ancients were hinting to us that the ultimate purpose of life is to expand our human minds until we realise the truth of the most expanded mind called, in Sanskrit, the *Brahman*, which is also the term for divinity.

In this sense, Hinduism is theistic, like Spinoza's God: divinity embedded within all entities and all entities embedded within the divine. Matter and consciousness are merely different expressions of the divine. As an outcome of this, Hinduism does not elevate equality as a virtue or as desirable. The equality paradigm views inequality as a problem because everyone is equal in the eyes of a monotheistic God. Hinduism, however, is comfortable with diversity and differences. It sees them as natural and varied expressions of the divine, depending on their respective karmic accumulations.

Since there is no concept of a monotheist God as creator, master and judge lording over His creations, it is only one's karmic actions that determine one's eventualities. And, since divinity is embedded in everything, wisdom lies in discovering the divinity in the other rather than engaging in judgement and condemnation.

Hinduism accommodates the world-renouncing form of God in Shiva as well as the world-embracing form of God in Vishnu. In addition to these two principles, the material world itself is said to be embodied in the form of the Goddess. Together, this trinity of beliefs shapes the central message of Hinduism: that the wise one *sees* underneath metaphysical diversities a common Unity and the epistemological perspective that this Unity can only be abstracted when one *sees* it in all of its diversity.

Hinduism advises that the way to navigate through these conflicting choices of renunciation or engagement or both in different contexts is to apply the principle of dharma in alignment with one's awareness of the self.

As we noted earlier, dharma can be understood as the law of identity. A thing is what it is. In the natural world, inanimate matter, plants and animals function according to their nature. A mango tree bears only the mango fruit.

Hence, if dharma is the law of identity, we can further deepen our understanding of karma as the law of identity put into action. When the Bhagavada Gita talks of Kurukshetra (the field of chosen action and consequences) as Dharmakshetra (the field of being who we really are), it is alluding to this interplay of the two principles. When one increases in wisdom and awareness of one's authentic self, one's actions will emerge in alignment with the self.

Indeed, Krishna stresses throughout the Bhagavad Gita that everyone should work according to their respective nature (*svadharma*), even if performed imperfectly. 'To follow another's path or to artificially suppress one's own authentic nature,' Krishna says, 'is dangerous and ill advised.'

As human beings, we are the only species with the capability to act against our nature, that is, act in non-dharmic ways. Every other living being acts for its own survival – either through consumption of food or through procreation. Both of these actions involve accruing karmic burden. Humans are the only creatures who can reject this natural survival instinct and minimise or avoid karmic accrual. Thus, we are faced with the choice of either renunciation or enlightened engagement (dharmic action) as the method of achieving liberation. Neither is the right way or the preferred path. Sometimes both are required in varying degrees in varying contexts, such as in the case of Ram – the incarnation of Vishnu – who renounces his kingdom and goes into exile only to return years later at the appropriate time and reclaim his kingdom.

Hinduism constantly moves across these boundaries of choices, actions and decisions. Another story that illustrates this preference for the liminal is of a demon who seeks immortality from the gods. He asks that he should not be killed by a man or a beast, indoors or outdoors, at day or at night. He makes his offerings and his wish is granted. The tale ends, however, with the demon being killed by Vishnu, a god who takes the form of Narasimha. The latter is both man and animal and the killing takes place on the threshold of a door that is neither indoors nor outdoors, and at twilight which is neither day nor night.

I Am Divine. So Are You.

Thus, great value is placed on the infinite spaces of wisdom between all kinds of boundaries. Hinduism celebrates these non-binary spaces. And, as it turns out, this is where the queer resides – indeed, where it thrives – in matters of sexuality, identity, and even beyond.

Coming Out

Karma performed with detachment, says Krishna in the Bhagavad Gita, is karma *yoga*, the *yoga* of action. In practice, this means being assertive without being arrogant. It means being firm about oneself, without being offensive to others. It means standing up not only for one's own rights and dignity but also for others like oneself and perhaps others who are struggling to have a voice. Taking part in community events, sharing and caring within the community and a relentless battle against the *adharma* of discrimination is one way of affirming one's faith. Hinduism advocates active engagement in the fight against negative feelings, which in today's world are forms of *adharma*.

In this way, 'coming out' would be a way to fight the negativity outside. And rejecting fear and loneliness would be a fight against negativity within oneself.

In the Mahabharata, Arjuna's well-known stint as the cross-dressing transgender Brihannala serves as a particularly notable example of the acceptance of third-gender people in ancient Hindu or Vedic society. Brihannala's traditional role as a skilled teacher of the fine arts and her acceptance by Maharaja Virata into his kingdom are all truly exemplary cases of affirming one's queer identity.

Dealing with Rejection

The *bhakti* scriptures emphasise qualities such as truthfulness, honesty, revealing one's mind in confidence, compassion, inclusiveness, and so on. Sri Isopanisad, one of the most ancient *bhakti* texts, declares: 'those who see the Supreme Lord within everything never hate anything nor any being'. The *Jaiva Dharma*, a more recent text compiled by Vaishnava visionary Bhaktivinoda Thakura, stresses that a Vaishnava 'does not adhere blindly to the rules and prohibitions of the scriptures but follows them only when they are favourable to his practice of *hari-bhajana* (worship of God). If they are unfavourable, he immediately rejects them.'

In this way, it can be interpreted, homosexuals and other third-gender people are not excluded from devotional culture but encouraged to embrace it in ways practical for them.

Contemporary spiritual leaders in India such as Sri Sri Ravi Shankar have publicly supported queer individuals, stating that nothing in Hinduism excludes homosexuality and nobody should face discrimination based on their sexual preferences. He said: 'Homosexuality is not a crime in any Smriti. Everyone has male and female elements. According to their dominance, tendencies show up and may change.'[15]

Conclusion

We must take into account that Hinduism is not monolithic and homogeneous. It comprises sects and communities variously identified as *sampradaya, parampara, pantha, vada* and *dera*. These are often led by charismatic spiritual leaders who insist that their followers obey a set of rules that distinguish them from others. These rules may often reflect the prejudices of the gurus themselves and may not be congruent with literatures and ideas that distinguish Hindu philosophy.

Yet, unlike Abrahamic faiths, the practice of Hinduism requires no endorsement from any authority (guru or book or institution or state). Everything boils down to social realities, rituals and, most importantly, the family. If the family is accepting, the queer person can find tremendous resources and support for emancipation.

The support of the faith and the state in conjunction with the family go a long way in affirming the dignity of queer people. However, even without that support, Hinduism offers a fluid, myriad world of diversity and beauty, where there is no judge and Judgement Day, no destination, and where liminal spaces thrive with unending possibilities. Those who can see the vastness of it all are called wise. Those who can't are nevertheless constituent elements of the divine.

Lord Krishna in this form, sporting plaited hair like a woman and expressing feminine grace with the tri-bent posture, as he enchants women of his village with his music, is referred to as the Complete Man *(purna-purusha)*, revealing how in embracing the feminine and masculine, the divine becomes complete.
(Photograph: Devdutt Pattanaik)

Appendix:
How to Conduct a Same-sex Wedding Based on Indian Rituals

By Devdutt Pattanaik

(Please note: These rituals cannot be considered as sanctioned by any religious authority. Also, same-sex relationships are not recognised by the state of India. Hence, conducting this ritual neither implies religious endorsement nor legal sanction.)

In Hinduism, gods and goddesses marry. Hindu temples routinely conduct wedding rituals of gods and goddesses with much pomp and revelry.

A wedding (*vivah*) in Hinduism is a rite of passage (*samskara*) that transforms a single entity into one half of a conjugal pair (*dampatya*). Being single, however, does not mean being incomplete. The idea of 'wholeness' in Hinduism is not necessarily a matter of the union of two bodies in marriage or even two souls in love; rather, wholeness or completeness in Hinduism can be understood as rising to the fullness of one's true self and expanding the arena of one's selfhood (*brah* – to expand, *manas* – the mind). Thus, even Krishna, visualised in a gentle, demure form with plaited hair and standing in a feminine pose, is considered the 'Complete Man' (*purna purusha*).

Hindu scriptures have no standard ceremony for marriages.

There are different types of marriages described in ancient texts – from a bride being given away by her father (*Prajapati vivah*) to a woman and man marrying in the presence of the natural elements with mutual consent (*Gandharva vivah*), to purchasing a bride (*Asura vivah*).

The rituals vary in different regions of India, and are different for different communities. These can be customised for a same-sex wedding.

Step 1
Making the proposal *(vara vinati)*

Elders or parents pay a visit to the parents of the spouse, offer them gifts and ask for the hand of their son or daughter in marriage for their son or daughter.

This ritual establishes that marriage is not only a union of individuals but also of families.

We [name] seek the hand of your son/daughter in marriage for our son/daughter [name].

Step 2
Accepting the proposal *(vara prapti)*

Elders accept the gifts and the proposal of marriage from the visiting family.

We [name] offer the hand of our son/daughter in marriage to your son/daughter [name].

I Am Divine. So Are You.

Step 3
Repeat with role reversal

In a typical heterosexual marriage, the groom's family asks for the bride's hand in marriage and the bride is offered by her family to the groom.

In a same-sex marriage, steps 1 and 2 will need to be repeated with a reversal of roles. These steps can be carried out with as much customisation and celebration as desired.

Step 4
Preparing for the wedding day *(mangal snan)*

The bride/groom bathe in fragrant water infused with the scents of flowers and wear clothes provided by the spouse's family.

Step 5
Invitation to the gods and guests *(devata avahana)*

On the wedding day, guests and gods are invited to gather around the sacred altar where the wedding ritual around the sacred fire will take place. Families can bring along images or statues of their personal deities to the ceremony.

Lamps are lit and flowers offered before the images of the personal deities of the families. If there are no deities, the lamp can be lit as representative of divinity.

Guests are offered garlands of flowers (marigold and rose) and sprinkled with perfumes or fragrant water.

Step 6

The arrival of the bride/groom *(vara preksha)*

The brides/grooms arrive separately at the ceremonial altar with their friends and family.

They are presented to each other, but their faces are covered with their hands; alternatively, a large leaf or a cloth is held between the brides/grooms as they face each other.

Gradually, their faces are uncovered and they are asked to see each other for the first time on this day. Conch shells, bells and music are played to celebrate the unveiling.

Step 7

Exchange of garlands *(vara mala)*

The brides/grooms exchange garlands.

> (Chanting)
> *This is a sacred symbol of my being. I give this to you, O auspicious one. May you and I live happily for a hundred years.*

Step 8

Exchange of rings/bracelet *(mangalya dharana)*

The brides/grooms exchange rings/bracelet.

> (Chanting)
> *This is a sacred symbol of my being. I give this to you, O auspicious one. May you and I live happily for a hundred years.*

I Am Divine. So Are You.

Step 9
Holding of hands *(pani grahan)*

The wedding couple now sit beside each other facing the sacred fire. The bride/groom extends his or her right palm to receive the right palm of the spouse. Elders and parents place flowers on the palm of the spouse that is held by the bride/groom. The flower is then offered to the gods symbolically by dropping the flowers before the images of the deities.

If deities are not present, the flower can be placed in front of the lit lamp or at the altar of the sacred fire.

This process is repeated with roles reversed.

Step 10
Tying of knot *(granthi bandhan)*

After the flowers are offered, elders place a stole or a shawl around the shoulders of the bride/groom and another on the shoulders of the spouse. They then tie the edges of the two stoles together into a knot.

Step 11
Touching the heart *(hriday sparsh)*

The bride/groom who is seated on the right wraps her/his left hand over the shoulder of the spouse in such a manner as to place his/her palm over the heart of the spouse.

While doing this, the bride/groom says, 'Grant me space in your heart forever.'

This is repeated with the roles reversed.

Step 12
Feeding each other *(anna prashana)*
The brides/grooms are offered sweets and delicacies, which they feed each other.

Step 13
Walking around the gods *(deva ashirwad)*
The brides/grooms stand up and one of them takes the lead to walk around the altar and the gods three times; the spouse follows the lead.

The roles are reversed and the three steps around the altar are taken again.

Step 14
Seven steps of togetherness *(sapta padi)*
The couple then take seven steps ahead together.

(Chanting)
By walking seven steps, let us pledge each other

1. *Time*
2. *Conversation*
3. *Pleasure*
4. *Loyalty*
5. *Support*
6. *Food*
7. *Wealth*

I Am Divine. So Are You.

Step 15

Bowing to the elders *(pitru-ashirwad)*

The couple return to their positions and, in unison, turn to each other's elders and take a bow.

Step 16

Shower of flowers *(pushpa-abhishek)*

Next, the couple bows before the guests.

At this time, the guests and family members shower the couple with flowers, petals or confetti to the sound of music

Everyone in unison chants, *'Mangal ho, mangal ho,'* which means 'May only good things happen, may only good things happen.'

The wedding ceremony is now complete.

Notes

1. Introduction to the Karmic Faiths

1   Patrick Olivelle (ed.), *Dharma: Studies in Its Semantic, Cultural and Religious History* (New Delhi: Motilal Banarsidass, 2004).

2   Muthuswami Dikshitar was a south Indian poet and composer and is one of the Musical Trinity of Carnatic music. He wrote the *Navagraha Kirtis*, in which he described the nine planets and identified Mercury as *napunsaka* (queer), as he was cursed to be so by the planet Jupiter.

3   Gayatri Reddy, *Colonialism and Criminal Castes with Respect to Sex: Negotiating Hijra Identity in South India* (Chicago: University of Chicago Press, 2005), pp. 26-27.

4   Tissy Mariam Thomas, *The Clan Culture of the Hijras: An Exploration into the Gender identity and Status of Hijras Inside and Outside Gharanas* (Bangalore: Centre for Research Projects, Christ University, 2013).

5   Sumit Guha, *Beyond Caste: Identity and Power in South Asia, Past and Present* (New Delhi: Permanent Black in association with Ashoka University, 2016).

6   The National Commission for Scheduled Tribes, Government of India, archived from the original on 14 Januuary 2012.

7   'Tribal Religions in India', http://factsanddetails.com/india/Religion_Caste_Folk_Beliefs_Death/sub7_2g/entry-4148.html, retrieved in September 2016.

8   'What are India's views regarding homosexuality?', https://www.quora.com/What-are-Indias-views-regarding-homosexuality, retrieved in September 2016.

9   John Powers, *A Bull of a Man: Images of Masculinity, Sex and the Body in Indian Buddhism* (London: Harvard University Press, 2009).

10 Ruth Vanita and Saleem Kidwai (eds.), *Same-sex Love in India: Readings from Literature and History* (New York: St Martin's Press, 2000).

11 Kumar Uttam, 'Modi asks BJP MPs to reach out to transgenders, seeks their 2-year report card', *Hindustan Times*, 10 August 2016, http://www.hindustantimes.com/india-news/modi-asks-bjp-mps-to-reach-out-to-transgenders-seeks-their-2-year-report-card/story-2CTEOmBYs1qAlPXdCilNgK.html.

2. Buddhism: Towards Liberation

1   'Cula-Malunkyovada Sutta: The Shorter Instructions to Malunkya (MN 63)', Access to Insight, accessed on 10 September 2016.

2   Pratapaditya Pal (ed.), *Buddhist Art, Form and Meaning* (New Delhi: Marg, 2007).

3   Mallar Ghosh, *Development of Buddhist Iconography in Eastern India* (Munshiram Manoharlal: 1980), p. 17.

4   Based on: Buswell Jr, Robert and Lopez Jr, Donald (eds.). *The Princeton Dictionary of Buddhism.* Oxford: Princeton University Press, 2014.

5   *Kama Sutta*, Sutta Nipata 4.1.

6   Vinaya Pitaka as quoted in http://www.fairobserver.com/region/asia_pacific/the-problem-with-sex-according-to-buddhism-10289/.

7   Ruth Vanita and Salim Kidwai (eds.), *Same Sex Love in India: A Literary History* (New Delhi: Penguin India, 2008), p. 19.

8   John Powers, *A Bull of a Man: Images of Masculinity, Sex and the Body in Indian Buddhism* (London: Harvard University Press, 2009).

9   'Gender Equality in Buddhism: How the Lotus Sutra Views the Enlightenment of Women', Soka Gakkai International: Buddhism in Action for Peace, http://www.sgi.org/about-us/president-ikedas-writings/a-grand-declaration-of-gender-equality.html.

10 Ruth Vanita and Salim Kidwai (eds.), *Same Sex Love in India: A Literary History* (New Delhi: Penguin India, 2008).

11 *The Collected Works (Gsun 'bum) of Yandgon-pa Rgyal-mtshan-dpal, Volume 2* (Thimphu: Kunsang Topgey, 1976), pp. 454-57 (cited in Gyatso 2003).

12 Paisarn Likhitpreechakul, 'Homophobic law has no basis in Buddhism', *The Nation*, 3 April 2015, http://www.nationmultimedia.com/opinion/Homophobic-law-has-NO-BASIS-in-Buddhism-30257329.html.

13 'Buddhism and sexual orientation', Wikipedia.org, https://en.wikipedia.org/wiki/Buddhism_and_sexual_orientation.

14 Ruth Vanita and Saleem Kidwai (eds.), *Same-sex Love in India: Readings from Literature and History* (New York: St Martin's Press, 2000).

15 John Powers, *A Bull of a Man: Images of Masculinity, Sex and the Body in Indian Buddhism* (London: Harvard University Press, 2009).

16 'Buddhism and sexual orientation', Wikipedia.org, https://en.wikipedia.org/wiki/Buddhism_and_sexual_orientation

17 Paisarn Likhitpreechakul, 'Homophobic law has no basis in Buddhism', *The Nation*, 3 April 2015, http://www.nationmultimedia.com/opinion/Homophobic-law-has-NO-BASIS-in-Buddhism-30257329.html.

18 Donald S. Lopez Jr (ed.), *Critical Terms for the Study of Buddhism* (Chicago: The University of Chicago Press, 2005).

19 'On Homosexuality and Sex in General', World Tibet Network News, 27 August 1997, http://www.tibet.ca/en/library/wtn/archive/old?y=1997&m=8&p=27-2_5.

20 Gary Leupp, *Male Colors: The Construction of Homosexuality in Tokugawa Japan* (California: University of California Press, 1997), p. 31.

21 P.D. Numrich, 'The Problem with Sex According to Buddhism', *Dialog*, Vol. 48, No. 1 (2009): pp. 62–73. doi:10.1111/j.1540-6385.2009.00431.x.

22 Dharmachari J'anavira, 'Homsexuality in the Japanese Buddhist Tradition', Western Buddhist Review, http://www.westernbuddhistreview.com/vol3/homosexuality.html#_ednref12.

23 Ibid.

24 Quoted directly from Jonathan Higbee, 'The Dalai Lama Approves Same-Sex Marriage, Says Bullying and Homophobia Is What's Wrong', Instinct Magazine, 27 February 2014, http://instinctmagazine.com/post/dalai-lama-approves-same-sex-marriage-says-bullying-and-homophobia-whats-wrong.

25 'Buddhism and sexual orientation', Wikipedia.org, https://en.wikipedia.org/wiki/Buddhism_and_sexual_orientation#cite_ref-58.

26 Ruth Vanita and Saleem Kidwai (eds.), *Same-sex Love in India: Readings from Literature and History* (New York: St Martin's Press, 2000).

27 Jeff Wilson, 'A Big Gay History of Same-sex Marriage in the Sangha', Tricycle.org, 27 June 2015, http://tricycle.org/trikedaily/big-gay-history-same-sex-marriage-sangha/.

28 Jeff Wilson, 'Jodo Shinshu Buddhism and Same-Sex Marriage in the United States', *Journal of Global Buddhism*, Vol. 13 (2012): pp. 31-59.

29 Barbara O'Brien, 'Did the Dalai Lama Endorse Gay Marriage?', Thoughtco.com, 26 June 2015, http://buddhism.about.com/od/Living-A-Buddhist-Life/fl/Same-Sex-Marriage-and-Buddhism.htm.

30 William Edelglass, 'Thich Nhat Hanh's Interbeing: Fourteen Guidelines for Engaged Buddhism' in William Edelglass and Jay L. Garfeild (eds.), *Buddhist Philosophy: Essential Readings* (Oxford: Oxford University Press, 2009), p. 420, 424.

31 'Karaniya Metta Sutta: The Buddha's Words on Loving-Kindness' (Sn 1.8), translated from the Pali by The Amaravati Sangha. Access to Insight (Legacy Edition), 2 November 2013, http://www.accesstoinsight.org/tipitaka/kn/snp/snp.1.08.amar.html.

3.   Jainism: A Quest for Non-violence

1   'Tirthankara', https://www.britannica.com/topic/Tirthankara, retrieved in
September 2016.

2   Kaliprasada Simha, *The Philosophy of Jainism* (Calcutta: Punthi Pustak, 1990).

4.   Sikhism: A Paradigm of Equality

1   'Mool Mantar', Sikhi Wiki: Encyclomedia of the Sikhs, retrieved in August 2016
http://www.sikhiwiki.org/index.php/Mool_Mantar.

2   Surinder Singh Johar, *Guru Nanak: A Biography* (California: New Book
Company, 1969).

3   'The Hindu Sacred Thread, Janeu', Sikhi Wiki: Encyclomedia of the Sikhs,
http://www.sikhiwiki.org/index.php/The_Hindu_Sacred_Thread,_Janeu,
retrieved in September 2016.

4   'There is no Hindu and no Musalman', Sikhi Wiki: Encyclomedia of the Sikhs,
http://www.sikhiwiki.org/index.php/There_is_no_Hindu_and_no_Musalman,
retrieved in September 2016.

5   J. Singh, 'Guru Nanak and the B40 Janamsakhi: The Meeting with Sheikh
Sharaf', Sarbat.net, 9 February 2009, http://www.sarbat.net/nanak-
b40janamsakhi.htm, retrieved in August 2016.

6   Sukhmandir Khalsa, 'The Four Laava: The Sikh Wedding Hymns', Thoughtco.
com, 18 September 2017, http://sikhism.about.com/od/sikhweddinghymns/a/
Lavan.htm.

7   Sukhdeep Singh, 'Religious Leaders Release Joint Statement Welcoming
Supreme Court Verdict on Sec 377', Gaylaxymag.com, 20 December 2013,
http://www.gaylaxymag.com/latest-news/religious-leaders-release-joint-
statement-welcoming-supreme-court-verdict-on-sec-377/.

8   'Sikh Head Priest Opposes Canada's Same-Sex Marriage Bill, Community
Opinion Split', UCANews.com, 3 February 2005, http://www.ucanews.com/
story-archive/?post_name=/2005/02/03/sikh-head-priest-opposes-canadas-
samesex-marriage-bill-community-opinion-split&post_id=25359.

9   Vivek Gupta and Aseem Bassi, 'Pro-gay Canadian leader runs into an
ethical wall in Punjab', *Hindustan Times*, 30 January 2016, http://www.
hindustantimes.com/punjab/sgpc-not-to-offer-siropa-to-lesbian-canada-
premier-at-golden-temple/story-nrz0hEBC699VnjxSLJHGpO.html.

10 Pat Johnson, 'Sikh Pride marshal reflects on difficulty coming out', *Vancouver
Courier*, 27 July 2016, http://www.vancourier.com/community/sikh-pride-
marshal-reflects-on-difficulty-coming-out-1.2311634.

5. Hinduism: The Wise See Diversity

1   Shrimad Bhagavad Gita, Chapter 7, verse 6.

2   Devdutt Pattanaik, *Shikhandi and Other Queer Tales They Don't Tell You* (New Delhi: Zubaan, 2014), p. 31.

3   Ibid.

4   Ibid, p. 121.

5   Devdutt Pattanaik, 'How a new akhara of transgendered people stole the spotlight at the Ujjain Kumbh', Scroll.in, 29 June 2016, https://scroll.in/article/809995/how-a-new-akhara-of-transgendered-people-stole-the-spotlight-at-the-ujjain-kumbh.

6   Wendy Doniger, *The Hindus: An Alternative History* (New Delhi: Penguin, 2009), p. 596.

7   Manusmriti (XI:175).

8   Louis-Georges Tin (ed.), *The Dictionary of Homophobia: A Global History of Gay & Lesbian Experience* (Vancouver: Arsenal, 2003).

9   Abhilash Rajendran, 'Adi Shankaracharya's Parakaya Pravesha to Learn Kamashastra', Hindu-blog.com, 12 July 2012, https://www.hindu-blog.com/2012/07/adi-shankaracharyas-parakaya-pravesha.html, retrieved in September 2016.

10 Gay and Lesbian Vaishnava Association: Information & Support for LGBTI Vaishnavas and Hindus, http://www.galva108.org/summary-of-vedic-references, retrieved in September 2016.

11 Gay and Lesbian Vaishnava Association: Information & Support for LGBTI Vaishnavas and Hindus, http://www.galva108.org/single-post/2014/05/11/Vedic-ThirdGender-Types-and-Terms.

12 James C. Harle, *The Art and Architecture of the Indian Subcontinent* (New Haven: Yale University Press, 1994), p. 161.

13 Gay and Lesbian Vaishnava Association: Information & Support for LGBTI Vaishnavas and Hindus, http://www.galva108.org/single-post/2014/05/11/Vedic-ThirdGender-Types-and-Terms.

14 Devdutt Pattanaik, *My Gita* (New Delhi: Penguin Random House, 2015).

15 'Homosexuality not a crime in Hinduism, says Sri Sri Ravi Shankar', FirstPost.com, 12 December 2013, http://www.firstpost.com/india/homosexuality-not-a-crime-in-hinduism-says-sri-sri-ravi-shankar-1283843.html.

Select Bibliography

1. Ambalal, Amit. *Krishna as Srinathji*. Ahmedabad: Mapin Publishing Pvt. Ltd, 1995.

2. Anderson, Leona M. *Vasantotsava: The Spring Festivals of India*. New Delhi: D.K. Printworld (P) Ltd, 1993.

3. Bagemihl, Bruce. *Biological Exuberance and Animal Homosexuality and Natural Diversity*. London: Profile Books, 1999.

4. Bhandarkar, Ramkrishna Gopal. *Vaisnavism, Saivism and Minor Religious Systems*. New Delhi: Asian Educational Services, 1983.

5. Bristow, Joseph. *Sexuality [The New Critical Idiom Series]*. London: Routledge, 1997.

6. Brown, Robert L, ed. *Ganesh – Studies of an Asian God*. Delhi: Sri Satguru, 1991.

7. Coupe, Lawrence. *Myth [The New Critical Idiom Series]*. London: Routledge, 1997.

8. Dange, Sadashiv Ambadas. *Encyclopaedia of Puranic Beliefs and Practices, Vol: 1–5*. New Delhi: Navran, 1990.

9. Danielou, Alan. *Gods of Love and Ecstasy: The Traditions of Shiva and Dionysus*. Rochester VT: Inner Traditions, 1992.

10. Devi, Shankuntala. *The World of Homosexuals*. New Delhi: Bell Books, 1978.

11. Dharwadker Vinay, ed. *The Collected Essays of A.K. Ramanujan*. New Delhi: Oxford University Press, 1999.

12. Doniger, Wendy and Smith, Brain K. *The Laws of Manu*. New Delhi: Penguin Books, 1991.

13. Doniger, Wendy. *Splitting the Difference*. New Delhi: Oxford University Press, 2000.

14. Eliot, Alexander. *The Universal Myths*. New York: Meridian Books, 1990.

15. Entwistle, A.W. *Braj, Centre of Krishna Pilgrimage*. Groningen, Netherlands: Egbert Forsten, 1987.

16. Flood, Gavin. *An Introduction to Hinduism*. New Delhi: Cambridge University Press, 1998.

17. Frawley, David. *From the River of Heaven*. New Delhi: Motilal Banarsidass Publishers Pvt. Ltd, 1992.

18. Graves, Robert. *The Greek Myths*. London: Penguin Books, 1960.

19. Hansen, Kathryn. *Grounds for Play: The Nautanki Theatre of North India*. Berkeley: University of California Press, 1991.

20. Hartsuiker, Dolf. *Sadhus, Holy Men of India*. London: Thames and Hudson, 1993.

21. Highwater, Jamake. *Myth & Sexuality*. New York: Meridian, 1990.

22. Hiltebeitel, Alf. *The Cult of Draupadi*. Chicago: The University of Chicago Press, 1988.

23. Jaini, Padmanabh S. *The Jaina Path of Purification*. New Delhi: Motilal Banarsidass Publishers Pvt. Ltd, 1979.

24. Jayakar, Pupul. *The Earth Mother*. New Delhi: Penguin Books, 1989.

25. Jordan, Michael. *Myths of the World*. London: Cambridge University Press, 1993.

26. Kakar, Sudhir. *The Inner World: A Psycho-analytic Study of Childhood and Society in India*. Delhi: Oxford University Press, 1981.

27. Kinsley, David. *Hindu Goddesses, Visions of the Divine Feminine in the Hindu Religious Tradition*. New Delhi: Motilal Banarsidass Publishers Pvt. Ltd, 1987.

28. Lorenzen, David and Munoz, Adrian, eds. *Yogi Heroes and Poets: Histories and Legends of the Naths*. New York: State University of New York Press, 2011.

29. Malhotra, Rajiv. *Indra's Net*. New Delhi: HarperCollins, 2014.

30. Mani, Vettam. *Puranic Encyclopaedia*. New Delhi: Motilal Banarsidass Publishers Pvt. Ltd, 1996.

31. Martin-Dubost, Paul. *Ganesha: Enchanter of the Three Worlds*. Mumbai: Franco-Indian Research, 1997.

32. Mazumdar, Subash. *Who is Who in the Mahabharata*. Mumbai: Bharatiya Vidya Bhavan, 1988.

33. Merchant, Hoshan, ed. *Yaraana: Gay Writing in India*. New Delhi: Penguin Books, 1999.

34. Meyer, Johann Jakob. *Sexual Life in Ancient India*. New Delhi: Motilal Banarsidass Publishers Pvt. Ltd, 1989.

35. Nabar V, Tumkur S, tr. *The Bhagavad Gita*. Hertfordshire: *Wordsworth Classics*, 1997.

36. Nagar, Shantilal & Naga, Tripta (translators). *Giradhara Ramayana in Gujarati*. Munshiram Manoharlal, 2003.

37. Nanda, Serena. *Neither Man Nor Woman: The Hijras of India*. Belmont, California: Wadsworth, 1990.

38. O'Flaherty, Wendy Doniger, tr. *The Rig Veda, an Anthology*. New Delhi: Penguin Books, 1994.

39. O'Flaherty, Wendy Doniger. *Sexual Metaphors and Animal Symbols in Indian Mythology*. New Delhi: Motilal Banarsidass Publishers Pvt. Ltd, 1981.

40. Panati, Charles. *Sexy Origins and Intimate Things*. New York: Penguin Books, 1998.

41. Randolph P., Lundschen Conner, David Hatfield Sparks, Mariya Sparks. *Cassell's Encyclopedia of Queer Myth, Symbol, and Spirit*. London: Cassel, 1997.

42. Schwartz, Kit. *The Male Member*. New York: St Martin's Press, 1985.

43. Sen, Makhan Lal. *The Ramayana of Valmiki*. New Delhi: Munishiram Manoharlal Publishers Pvt. Ltd, 1978.

44. Spencer, Colin. *Homosexuality, a History*. London: Fourth Estate, 1995.

45. Staal, Frits. *Discovering the Vedas: Origins, Mantras, Rituals, Insights*. New Delhi: Penguin India, 2008.

46. Subramaniam, Kamala. *Mahabharata*. Mumbai: Bharatiya Vidya Bhavan, 1988.

47. Subramaniam, Kamala. *Ramayana*. Mumbai: Bharatiya Vidya Bhavan, 1990.

48. Subramaniam, Kamala. *Srimad Bhagavatam*. Mumbai: Bharatiya Vidya Bhavan, 1987.

49. Thadani, Giti. *Sakhiyani*. London: Cassell, 1996.

50. Vanita, Ruth, and Kidwai, Salim, eds. *Same Sex Love in India: A Literary History*. New Delhi: Penguin India, 2008.

51. Varma, Pavan K. *Krishna, the Playful Divine*. New Delhi: Penguin Books, 1993.

52. Walker, Benajmin. *Hindu World, Vol. 1 & 2*. New Delhi: Munishiram Manoharlal Publishers Pvt. Ltd, 1983.

53. Wilhelm, Amara Das. *Tritiya-Prakriti: People of the Third Sex*. Philadelphia: Xlibris Corporation, 2003.

54. Zimmer, Heinrich. *Myths and Symbols in Indian Art and Civilization*. New Delhi: Motilal Banarsidass Publishers Pvt. Ltd, 1990.

Index

perception of queer, 32–33
primary conflict in, 8–9
representation of genders, 18
scripture or intellectual analysis, 30–32
transformation of the world, 16–19
view on society, 5
words for queer in texts, 18
Kharavela, King, 74
King, Larry, 58
kinnara, 14, 18, 37, 125
kliba, 14, 18, 127, 130
Kooboo Daishi (Kuukai), 58
Kshatriyas, 26, 92
Kurundi Atthakatha, 53

L

LGBTIQ people, 2. *see also* queer, representation of
liberation, 6
Lingayats, 28
linguistic division of states, India, 24
Lotus Sutra, 53
love or loving kindness *(metta)*, 65

M

Mahabharata, 26, 112, 121
Mahakala Ma Ning, God, 51
Mahavira, 73–74
Mahavira, Lord, 8
Mahayana Buddhism, 43–46
Malli-natha, Tirthankara, 81
manas, 17
Mangal-mukhi community, 125
Manimekhalai, 50
man-like woman *(vepurisika)*, 49
Manusmriti, 27, 34
'*matsya nyaya*' or 'justice of the fishes', 17–18
matter *(mudgala)*, 16
maya, 6
metaphysical monism, 45
Mimamsa school of thought, 10
Modi, Narendra, 37
moha, 6
moksha, 12, 114
Mulachar of Vattakera, 77

N

Nagarjuna, 50
Nanak, Guru, 90–94, 99
napunsaka, 14
nirvana, 12, 17, 49

O

Oriental faiths, 5

P

Padmavati, demigoddess, 84
Pakistan, 24
Pali Tipitaka, 50
pandaka, 14
pandakas, 51–54
Pulakesin Chalukya, King, 74

Q

queer, representation of
in Ayurveda, 18
dignity of queer people, 35–38
in Hinduism, 33
in Hinduism, 32–33, 126, 130–35
interpretation in *jyotisha*, 18–19
in Jainism, 33
in Karmic faiths, 18, 32–34
Karmic faiths hostility to queer, 34
marriage between queers, 36
queer themes in stories, 32–33
in Sikhism, 101–2, 105–6
transgender identities of Gods, 33
queer *pandaka*, 34
queer-phobia, 2

R

Ramakrishna Mission, 111
Ramayana, 26, 112, 122–23
Ram Das, Guru, 91, 102
Rashtriya Swayamsevak Sangh, 28
rebirth, idea of, 3
Reformation, 14
religious belief systems, 111
Renaissance, 14
Rig Veda, 26
ritual 'purity', 12
river of materiality, 16–17
Roman Empire, 13